105 QUESTIONS CHILDREN ASK ABOUT MONEY MATTERS

105 Questions Children Ask about money matters

with answers from the Bible for busy parents

General Editor:
Daryl J. Lucas

Contributors:
David R. Veerman, M.Div.
James C. Galvin, Ed.D.
James C. Wilhoit, Ph.D.
Bruce B. Barton, D.Min.
Richard Osborne
Jonathan Farrar

Illustrator:
Lil Crump

Tyndale House Publishers, Inc. Wheaton, Illinois

Visit Tyndale's exciting Web site at www.tyndale.com

© 1997 by The Livingstone Corporation and Lightwave Publishing, Inc.
All rights reserved.

Illustrations by Lil Crump. "Jason and Max" © 1989 by Impartation Idea,
Inc. All rights reserved.

Produced for Tyndale by Lightwave Publishing and The Livingstone
Corporation. Bruce B. Barton, James C. Galvin, David R. Veerman, Daryl
J. Lucas, Jonathan Farrar, Livingstone project staff.

Scripture quotations are taken from the *Holy Bible,* New Living
Translation, copyright © 1996. Used by permission of Tyndale House
Publishers, Inc., Wheaton, Illinois 60189. All rights reserved.

Library of Congress Cataloging-in-Publication Data

105 questions children ask about money matters / general editor, Daryl J.
Lucas ; contributors, David R. Veerman . . . [et al.]; illustrator, Lil Crump.
   p. cm.
  ISBN 0-8423-4526-4 (sc)
  1. Children—Finance, Personal. 2. Finance, Personal—Religious
aspects—Christianity. 3. Money—Religious aspects—Christianity.
4. Finance, Personal—Biblical teaching. 5. Money—Biblical teaching.
I. Lucas, Daryl. II. Veerman, David.
HG179.A16 1997
332.024—dc21   97-951

Printed in the United States of America

03 02 01 00 99 98 97
7   6   5   4   3   2   1

CONTENTS

LIVING AND GIVING

FOREWORD BY LARRY BURKETT

This is a book that's long overdue. There has been a need, since probably the late 1950s, to train children in the area of finances. However, in 1973, when I began teaching on biblical principles for handling finances, there were no books available to teach people how to manage their finances according to God's Word. As a result, I concentrated all of my efforts on studying the Bible and developing the materials to help families manage their finances properly as good stewards.

I recognized immediately how necessary it is to begin financial training at an early age. I think back to my own childhood: At twelve years old I was making a living and thinking pretty much like an adult. That wasn't unusual for a twelve-year-old in the 1950s. Simply put, my parents said, "You can have whatever you want, as long as you earn it and you're able to afford it on your own." That was great motivation for me.

Remember two things: One, you're not actually teaching *children;* you are teaching *future adults* things they need to know in order to survive in the society we have created for them. And two, if you're just giving them your *opinion,* whatever you can talk them into, some slick-talking person may try to talk them out of. One of the things I learned a long time ago, both about other people and about myself and my family, is that if I could talk someone into something, someone else might come along behind me and talk them out of it. But whatever I could share with them from God's Word, *nobody* would ever be able to talk them out of.

As a result of that simple philosophy, I began to see people who were getting their finances squared away and getting themselves out of financial bondage. I believe this same philosophy can be applied as you teach your children.

We should be concerned about what our children are learning when no one is overtly teaching them. They are smart enough to listen and decipher information that is presented to them. However, if you can instill in your children the biblical principles of handling money, and if you can do it in a manner they will understand, that is God's best for their lives. Then you'll discover that over the long run the principles you instill in them will be there forever.

I trust this book will be a blessing to many people because I believe it deals with what is perhaps the most vital topic in America today. We suffer from a lack of morality, a lack of ethics, and a lack of discipline in our country—in every area. However, in no area is the lack more visible and more acute than in the area of money.

I pray that God will use this book to help ensure a better future for your children. God bless you.

—Larry Burkett

Lauree and L. Allen Burkett are cofounders of Money Matters for Kids. Their vision is to help children understand biblical principles of stewardship God's way through fun and innovative products and programs. Be sure to look for the "Money Matters for Kids" seal of quality on children's financial products.

NOTE FROM THE WRITERS

Children soon learn the value of a buck. The first few times it buys them a candy bar or a toy, the lesson of capitalism sinks in: If you have money, you can get stuff.

Almost everything else they learn about money will need refinement. They won't learn to tithe all by themselves. They won't learn to save just because they have enough to set aside. They won't understand the dangers of borrowing the instant they can write an IOU. And they surely won't fathom why Mom and Dad say, "We can't afford it."

Hence the questions. We collected hundreds of them, selected the most common and important, and sorted them into categories. If you are a parent of children ages 3 to 10 or if you work with children, you have surely heard questions like these—or soon will.

For every question, we identified Bible passages that speak to it, then summarized their application to that question. Study the Scriptures listed with the questions because the Bible has a lot to say about how we use money. It doesn't answer every question directly, but it gives many principles that every Christian should know and live by.

As you answer children's questions, keep the following points in mind:

1. "Silly" questions are serious questions. Always take children's questions seriously. Don't laugh at them. Some questions may sound silly to you, but they're not silly to your child. Be careful not to ridicule your child's ideas.

2. Some questions hide fears or insecurities. When a child asks, "Why does God sometimes wait until the last minute to supply our needs?" (question 28), she's looking for reassurance. She has felt the anxiety of having little, or she's picked it up from her parents, and she's afraid. She wants assurance that God will take care of her. Go ahead and answer "the question behind the question": Assure your child that God will always meet her needs. If you suspect that there is a hidden question but don't know what it is, a great way to get at it is to ask, "Why do you ask?" or "Why do you want to know?"

3. The best answers come from Scripture. The Bible doesn't answer every curiosity we have, but it does have many important guidelines for the use of money. Study the Scriptures listed with each answer, including any related verses.

4. The best answers avoid theological jargon. Use normal words. Children think in terms of their own experiences, so abstract concepts don't mean a thing to them. As much as possible, talk about *things, events,* and *objects* they can imagine. Talk about an *action,* such as buying a toy. Give them something to look at in their mind. If they can imagine it, they are more likely to understand it.

5. Some questions have no answer. Be careful not to make up an answer when you don't have one and when the Bible is silent. If you don't have an answer, say so. Or suggest that you look for the answer together. Emphasize the truths and guidelines of Scripture that you *do* know.

6. Some kids just want to keep asking. Be ready for follow-up questions and be willing to keep talking. Your answer may lead to more questions. That's the mark of a good answer—it makes the child think.

We wrote this book to help you answer kids' questions about money matters. We sincerely hope and pray it does that.

—Dave Veerman, Jim Galvin, Jim Wilhoit, Bruce Barton, Daryl Lucas, Rick Osborne, Jon Farrar, Lil Crump

MONEY DOESN'T GROW ON TREES

Q: WHERE DOES MONEY COME FROM, GOD OR PEOPLE?

A: The Bible says that in the very beginning, God created the heavens and the earth (Genesis 1:1) and that everything was made by him (John 1:3). So everything there is came from God. The sun, moon, oceans, trees, animals, sky, and land all came from him. The Bible also says, "Whatever is good and perfect comes to us from God above" (James 1:17). But this doesn't mean that God makes every little thing in the world himself. Instead, he expects people to use the materials he has given them to make things like bread, cars, toys, medicine, houses, clothes, and money. God made the world and people, and he makes it all work right. You might say that money comes *from* God *through* people. But God doesn't make money—*people* print money and mint coins. God enables people to earn and use it.

God makes it possible for people to earn money. He made people. He made their skills. He made the bosses. He controls the world.

KEY VERSE: *It is a good thing to receive wealth from God and the good health to enjoy it. To enjoy your work and accept your lot in life—that is indeed a gift from God. (Ecclesiastes 5:19)*

RELATED VERSES: *Psalm 50:10; 111:5; Matthew 6:19-34; 19:21-24*

RELATED QUESTIONS: *If money doesn't grow on trees, where does it come from? Why did God make money?*

NOTE TO PARENTS: *This assumes money comes either from God or from people. Emphasize the important role of both by thanking God for what you have and for the people through whom it comes.*

Q: WHY IS THERE SUCH A THING AS MONEY?

A: People use money to trade one thing for another. Think about when you go to the store. If you want to get something in the store, how would you do that without money? You would have to trade something for what you want in the store, and the store would have to want what you have to trade. That might get very complicated. That's why there is money—it's something that everyone can use for trade.

KEY VERSE: *The king replied to Araunah, "No, I insist on buying it, for I cannot present burnt offerings to the Lord my God that have cost me nothing." So David paid him fifty pieces of silver for the threshing floor and the oxen. (2 Samuel 24:24)*

RELATED VERSES: *Genesis 42:35; 2 Kings 12:5; Ecclesiastes 5:19; Isaiah 30:6*

RELATED QUESTIONS: *How did money start? If everything was free, then the world would be a better place, so why did people make money in the first place?*

Q: WHY DON'T PEOPLE JUST TRADE FOR WHAT THEY NEED?

A: Long ago (and in some places even today) people traded *things* with each other instead of using money. They traded food they grew, animals they raised, things they made, and so forth. For example, someone might trade some grain for a table. Or someone might trade a cow for shoes and clothes. But this only worked if each of the traders wanted what the other had to trade. If you had only a model airplane to trade and no one else wanted it, you wouldn't be able to get what you needed. Money makes trading easier because everybody can use it. If you trade money for a new model airplane, the person who sold it to you can use the money to trade for a baseball glove. Money makes trading easy.

KEY VERSE: *Joseph collected all the money in Egypt and Canaan in exchange for grain, and he brought the money to Pharaoh's treasure-house. (Genesis 47:14)*

RELATED VERSES: *Genesis 13:2; 34:10*

RELATED QUESTION: *What did people do before money came?*

Q: WHEN WAS MONEY INVENTED?

A: Money was invented many thousands of years ago. We know that early Egyptian civilizations traded precious minerals, for example. In Old Testament times, people traded gold and silver by its weight, rather than using coins. By New Testament times, people throughout the Roman Empire used coins to buy and sell.

KEY VERSES: *So they left Egypt and traveled north into the Negev—Abram with his wife and Lot and all that they owned, for Abram was very rich in livestock, silver, and gold. (Genesis 13:1-2)*

RELATED VERSES: *Genesis 2:11-12*

RELATED QUESTIONS: *When did money start, and why? Who invented money? Who made up the idea of money?*

Q: WHY ARE THOSE LITTLE PIECES OF PAPER WORTH SO MUCH?

A: It may seem strange that a little piece of paper, like a dollar bill, is worth so much. Actually, the paper itself isn't worth very much at all. The paper of a one-dollar bill is worth less than a penny. But the one-dollar bill has worth because the government says it does. It is worth 100 pennies.

The federal government says how much each special piece of paper is worth. And only the government can print money. If you drew your own money on paper, it wouldn't be worth anything, even if you said it was.

KEY VERSES: *"Here, show me the Roman coin used for the tax." When they handed him the coin, he asked, "Whose picture and title are stamped on it?" "Caesar's," they replied. "Well, then," he said, "give to Caesar what belongs to him. But everything that belongs to God must be given to God." (Matthew 22:19-21)*

RELATED VERSES: *Job 28:15-19*

RELATED QUESTION: *What does "means of exchange" mean?*

Q: WHY ARE THERE ALL DIFFERENT KINDS OF MONEY?

A: One reason is that each country makes its own money. Other differences come from different denominations of money. Coins and bills are made with different values so money will be easy to manage. If the only kind of money were the penny, you would have to carry bags and bags of pennies to buy groceries.

Some people have a lot of fun collecting different kinds of money. They make a hobby of collecting coins and bills from all over the world and from different times in history.

KEY VERSES: *[The Pharisees asked,] "Now tell us what you think about this: Is it right to pay taxes to the Roman government or not?" But Jesus knew their evil motives. "You hypocrites!" he said. "Whom are you trying to fool with your trick questions? Here, show me the Roman coin used for the tax." When they handed him the coin, he asked, "Whose picture and title are stamped on it?" "Caesar's," they replied. "Well, then," he said, "give to Caesar what belongs to him. But everything that belongs to God must be given to God." (Matthew 22:17-21)*

RELATED VERSE: *1 Kings 10:10*

RELATED QUESTIONS: *How does money work? How does the country's money system work?*

NOTE TO PARENTS: *If your child shows a lot of interest in this, you could start a collection of different types of money from different countries. You could even use the money as a way of studying those countries' cultures.*

Q: WHERE DOES THE MONEY GO WHEN YOU BUY WHAT YOU WANT?

7

A: When you give money to a store owner or a salesperson, that person puts it in a safe place, such as a drawer, a safe, or a bank. Later the store owner can use the money to pay the employees and to pay for things he or she wants. The employees then go out and buy things that they want. And the store owners who get those dollars do the same thing with the money they get.

Let's say you give Mr. Jones a dollar to buy a toy you want. Later, Mr. Jones uses that dollar to buy a stamp at the post office. Then the postal clerk gives the dollar to Mrs. Smith as change. Mrs. Smith goes home and gives her son the dollar for his allowance. The money just keeps going from person to person!

KEY VERSE: *When she told the man of God what had happened, he said to her, "Now sell the olive oil and pay your debts, and there will be enough money left over to support you and your sons." (2 Kings 4:7)*

RELATED VERSE: *Proverbs 14:23*

RELATED QUESTIONS: *When you buy with a check, what does the person you gave the check to do with it? What happens after you give someone a check?*

NOTE TO PARENTS: *It's not immediately obvious where money goes when you buy something, so this is a logical question. Just try to explain that it simply changes hands. One person gives it to another.*

Q: WHY ISN'T A DOLLAR WORTH A DOLLAR ANYMORE?

8

A: When people say that a dollar isn't worth a dollar anymore, they mean that a dollar doesn't buy as much in a store as it used to. Let's say that ten years ago a dollar bought ten chocolate chip cookies. But today when you go to the store you only get seven cookies for your dollar. You would be getting less for your money than you used to.

This happens for many reasons, but it's a little like a circle of dominoes. The store owner, the baker, the chocolate-chip maker, and the cocoa-bean farmer are all dominoes in the circle. If a hurricane wipes out part of the cocoa-bean crop, the cocoa-bean farmer has to raise his prices. The chocolate-chip maker has to pay more for cocoa, so he then has to raise *his* prices. The baker has to pay more for chocolate chips, so he has to raise *his* prices. And the store owner has to pay more for cookies, so he has to raise *his* prices. It is not always that simple, but that's one reason prices go up.

Don't worry about it, though. No matter what a dollar is worth, God is in control, and we can trust him to take care of us.

KEY VERSE: *The Lord will not let the godly starve to death, but he refuses to satisfy the craving of the wicked. (Proverbs 10:3)*

RELATED VERSES: *1 Kings 10:29; Proverbs 11:28; Ezekiel 7:19*

RELATED QUESTION: *Why did prices inflate so much from what they used to be?*

YOU CAN
BANK ON IT

Q: WHY DO WE PUT OUR MONEY IN THE BANK WHEN WE HAVE TO KEEP GOING BACK THERE TO GET IT?

9

A: The main reason that people put money in banks is for safety. At home you can lose your money or someone can steal it. But it is very difficult to steal from a bank.

It's also easier to keep your money in a bank than to keep it all in your house or in your pocket. Banks are safe and easy to use.

Banks also pay you a little bit when you save your money there. That's called interest.

KEY VERSES: *The master replied, "You wicked and lazy servant! You think I'm a hard man, do you, harvesting crops I didn't plant and gathering crops I didn't cultivate? Well, you should at least have put my money into the bank so I could have some interest." (Matthew 25:26-27)*

RELATED QUESTIONS: *Why do we have banks when they just get robbed? Why can't we just keep our money at home?*

NOTE TO PARENTS: *Children who are old enough to have their own bank accounts are still years away from being able to get to their money without your help. It's a good idea to let them keep enough of their spending money at home that they are not frustrated by this.*

Q: HOW MUCH MONEY ARE WE SUPPOSED TO PUT IN THE BANK?

10

A: You don't *have* to put any money in the bank. The Bible doesn't tell us that people have to put their money in banks. But putting money in the bank is a good idea.

When you put money in the bank, you are saving it for later. You should decide first what it is you want to save for. Maybe you want to save up for a special toy, a campout with the youth group, or college. Once you know what you're saving for, you can figure out how much money you need to put in the bank each week or each month so you will have enough for what you want when the time comes.

KEY VERSES: *"You wicked servant!" the king roared. "Hard, am I? If you knew so much about me and how tough I am, why didn't you deposit the money in the bank so I could at least get some interest on it?" (Luke 19:22-23)*

RELATED VERSE: *Proverbs 21:20*

RELATED QUESTIONS: *Why should we save money? If you have only five dollars in the bank, will the bankers kick you out? How do you make sure you have enough money in the bank to cover a check?*

NOTE TO PARENTS: *Take this sort of question as an opportunity to talk about budgeting. Children should have savings goals and work toward them, even if the goals are small. Help your child identify these goals, write them down, and save up little by little. This will illustrate the wisdom of saving money, the reasons for saving, and the power of choice.*

Q:

WHY DO WE HAVE TO PUT MONEY IN THE BANK WHEN WE HAVE OUR OWN PIGGY BANKS?

11

A: A bank lets you do a lot more with your money than just store it. If someone has money in the bank, he or she can write checks, get small amounts of money out as it is needed, and pay bills from the money in the bank.

A bank has other benefits too. It pays you a little bit for keeping your money, it keeps the money safe, and it can hold as much as you'll ever get. It's fun to put money in a piggy bank. But sooner or later you'll want to have a bank account.

KEY VERSE: *Guard these treasures well until you present them, without an ounce lost, to the leading priests, the Levites, and the leaders of Israel at the storerooms of the Lord's Temple in Jerusalem. (Ezra 8:29)*

RELATED VERSES: *Matthew 6:19-20; Luke 19:23*

RELATED QUESTIONS: *Why is it so good to put money in the bank? Why don't people keep their money in a piggy bank?*

NOTE TO PARENTS: *A young child has no idea how much money passes through an adult's checking account, so a child might think,* If I can keep my money in a piggy bank, why can't you? *Explain to your children that you have to keep track of much more money than they do. You might even want to show your children your monthly budget and your plan to meet all your commitments. You can also point out the bank systems that help you do this.*

Q: WHAT DOES THE BANK DO WITH EVERYONE'S MONEY?

12

A: They put some of it in a vault and loan a lot of it to others. They don't need to keep everyone's money in a separate place. And they don't even need to keep all of it in the vault. They just need to have enough to give to anyone who comes to get some of his or her money out. The bank keeps track of everybody's money through its computer system.

A bank is a business that makes money by loaning money to others. Here's how it works. A lot of people put money in the bank. Then the bank loans some of the money to other people. For example, most people who want to buy a house borrow money from a bank. The people who borrow the money pay it back plus a little more. The extra that they pay is called interest. The more loans the bank makes, the more people pay interest, and the more money the bank makes.

KEY VERSES: *The master replied, "You wicked and lazy servant! You think I'm a hard man, do you, harvesting crops I didn't plant and gathering crops I didn't cultivate? Well, you should at least have put my money into the bank so I could have some interest." (Matthew 25:26-27)*

RELATED QUESTIONS: *How do bankers organize your money? How do banks keep everybody's money at the same time?*

Q: WHAT HAPPENS TO MY MONEY IF THE BANK GETS ROBBED?

13

A: Don't worry about your money in the bank. It's safe. Very few banks get robbed, and most bank robbers get caught. The few thieves who get away get very little money. Also, the money in the bank is insured. The government guarantees that even if someone stole all the money in the bank, you would still get yours back.

KEY VERSES: *[Jesus said,] "Don't store up treasures here on earth, where they can be eaten by moths and get rusty, and where thieves break in and steal. Store your treasures in heaven, where they will never become moth-eaten or rusty and where they will be safe from thieves." (Matthew 6:19-20)*

RELATED QUESTIONS: *If your money in the bank gets stolen, will the bank make it up to you? Why would you put your money in a bank when there's so much robbery?*

NOTE TO PARENTS: *Children tend to believe horror stories, especially stories about bank robberies. Assure your child that a bank is a safe place to put money. Because of tight security, many bank robbers take a very small percentage of the money actually in the bank. Also remind your child that our ultimate trust is in God, not the bank. In 1929, those who trusted in American banks did suffer losses, but God did not abandon his people.*

Q: WHY DO BANKS GIVE INTEREST?

14

A: Interest is a small payment you get for putting your money in the bank. The bank wants you to let it keep your money so it can loan the money to others. To get you to do this, the bank pays you a little bit for leaving your money there. The bank pays you interest.

Why does the bank want to loan money to others? So it can make money. The people who borrow money from the bank have to pay interest on their loans. The more the bank has to loan, the more interest payments it can collect.

It's OK for a bank to charge interest because that's how it makes money. But we should not treat our family and friends that way. In Old Testament times, God did not allow his people to charge each other interest. They were to loan money without charging for it.

KEY VERSES: *"You wicked servant!" the king roared. "Hard, am I? If you knew so much about me and how tough I am, why didn't you deposit the money in the bank so I could at least get some interest on it?" (Luke 19:22-23)*

RELATED VERSE: *Deuteronomy 23:20*

RELATED QUESTIONS: *Why is there more money in my bank account than what I put in? When we put money in banks, the bank should pay us more, shouldn't it?*

NOTE TO PARENTS: *You can demonstrate the way interest works by giving your child money to buy candy. Pretend you are a bank and are loaning the money to him. He will have to pay it all back plus a penny if he pays you tomorrow, a nickel if he pays in a week, and so on. Whoever the money belongs to gets to collect the interest.*

Q: WHAT ARE ACCOUNTS?

15

A: An account is a place to put your money in a bank. The money is set aside just for you. An account is like a piggy bank or an envelope with your name on it at the bank. It's a way for the bank to keep track of your money.

Your parents, friends, and many other people also have money in the bank. The bank keeps track of each person's money by using accounts. If three of your friends gave you some money to keep for them, you could keep it in three separate places. Another way would be to write on a piece of paper how much each person had given to you. Then you could put all the money in one place. That's how accounts work at a bank. All the money is put together, but the bank has a record of how much of *your* money they have.

KEY VERSE: *They gave Hilkiah the high priest the money that had been collected by the Levites who served as gatekeepers at the Temple of God. The gifts were brought by people from Manasseh, Ephraim, and from all the remnant of Israel, as well as from all Judah, Benjamin, and the people of Jerusalem. (2 Chronicles 34:9)*

RELATED VERSE: *Proverbs 22:7*

RELATED QUESTIONS: *Where does the money go? Do you need to have a bank account when you're older?*

NOTE TO PARENTS: *You can explain that a bank account is like a piggy bank at home, except that the bank pays you and can hold a lot more. You might even get out the Monopoly money and play "bank." You can illustrate a lot and have fun as well.*

Q: HOW CAN WE BUY THINGS WITH A CHECK INSTEAD OF MONEY?

ice cream

16

A: A check is a set of instructions to the bank to pay money from a person's account to someone else. If you look closely at a check you will see the words *Pay to the order of* and then a blank line. This line is a message to the bank; it means, "When the person named on this line asks for the amount of money written on this check, go ahead and pay the person, and take the money from my account." There is a place for the person who wrote the check to sign it to show that the check is real.

Checks are more convenient than cash. A check allows you to pay someone without having to go to the bank or carry a lot of money with you.

Checks are also safer than cash. If you lose cash, anyone can use it. But a check can only be cashed by the person you wrote it to. That's why people send checks—not cash—through the mail.

KEY VERSES: *I also said to the king, "If it please Your Majesty, give me letters to the governors of the province west of the Euphrates River, instructing them to let me travel safely through their territories on my way to Judah. And please send a letter to Asaph, the manager of the king's forest, instructing him to give me timber. I will need it to make beams for the gates of the Temple fortress, for the city walls, and for a house for myself." And the king granted these requests, because the gracious hand of God was on me. (Nehemiah 2:7-8)*

RELATED QUESTION: *How does a checking account work?*

NOTE TO PARENTS: *Write a check the next time you give your child money. Then take your child to the bank to cash it.*

Q: HOW DOES A CHECK BOUNCE?

17

A: The word *bounce* describes what happens when a person writes a check for more money than he or she has in the bank. A check is a set of instructions to the bank that says, "Pay this amount of money to the person named on this check." If there's not enough money in the account, the bank won't follow the instructions. It won't cash the check. The bank says, "This person doesn't have enough money to cover this check" and returns the check. It "bounces" back.

A check is a promise. Just as we should always keep our spoken promises, so we should always make sure we have enough money in the bank to cover the checks we write. It is dishonest to write a check when we know we don't have enough money to cover it.

KEY VERSES: *Who would begin construction of a building without first getting estimates and then checking to see if there is enough money to pay the bills? Otherwise, you might complete only the foundation before running out of funds. And then how everyone would laugh at you! They would say, "There's the person who started that building and ran out of money before it was finished!" (Luke 14:28-30)*

RELATED VERSES: *Proverbs 12:17; 16:11*

RELATED QUESTION: *Why do some stores not take checks?*

Q: WHERE DOES ALL THE MONEY IN THE BANK MACHINES COME FROM?

18

A: Bank workers put it there. About once a week they open the machines (called automatic teller machines, or ATMs) and put the money in. They get the money from the bank's safe. The bank workers put enough into the machines so whoever needs to get some from their account can do so.

KEY VERSES: *Joash gave instructions for a chest to be made and set outside the gate leading to the Temple of the Lord. Then a proclamation was sent throughout Judah and Jerusalem, telling the people to bring to the Lord the tax that Moses, the servant of God, had required of the Israelites in the wilderness. This pleased all the leaders and the people, and they gladly brought their money and filled the chest with it. (2 Chronicles 24:8-10)*

RELATED VERSES: *Proverbs 21:20, 25*

RELATED QUESTION: *Do bank machines get robbed?*

NOTE TO PARENTS: *Younger children often get the impression from watching adults use automatic teller machines that you can get money whenever you want and get as much as you want. Explain that using an ATM is like getting money out of your piggy bank. You are getting out money that you had put in earlier. Older children can benefit from having and using an ATM card. It can be very convenient for them and for you, and it can give them practice managing their own money.*

IN GOD
WE TRUST

Q: IS IT ALL RIGHT TO PRAY TO GOD FOR MONEY?

19

A: Yes, it is fine and good to pray to God about money and to ask him for money. The Bible tells Christians to "pray about everything" (Philippians 4:6), that "whatever is good and perfect comes to us from God" (James 1:17), and that "the reason you don't have what you want is that you don't ask God for it" (James 4:2). God *wants* you to know this, and there is no better person to ask than God whenever you need anything, including money. You *should* ask God for the money you need.

Just think carefully about what you want the money for. God promises to provide what we need. But Jesus warned against greed and love for money. God won't give you money to get something just because you want it badly.

KEY VERSE: *This same God who takes care of me will supply all your needs from his glorious riches, which have been given to us in Christ Jesus. (Philippians 4:19)*

RELATED VERSES: *Matthew 6:11; 7:7; 1 Timothy 6:10; Hebrews 13:5; James 2:15-16; 4:1-3*

RELATED QUESTION: *How does God supply money?*

NOTE TO PARENTS: *Whenever you pray for money as a family, thank God for the jobs, gifts, and other sources of income he has already provided. Remember to show your thankfulness even when you need more.*

Q: HOW DO I TRUST GOD FOR MONEY?

20

A: First, pray. Tell God what you need, what you would like, and how you feel. But also tell him that you trust him to take care of you and to do what is best for you. Then put your mind at ease and do not worry. God promises to provide for his people. He also tells us to be content with what we have. You can be sure that God is doing what is best for you.

KEY VERSE: *[Jesus said,] "Don't be troubled. You trust God, now trust in me." (John 14:1)*

RELATED VERSES: *Psalm 125:1; 138:7-8; Proverbs 3:5*

RELATED QUESTIONS: *What should you do if you can't find a job? Trusting God for money—does it mean to let him bring in work, or trust that he'll lead you to work?*

NOTE TO PARENTS: *You can demonstrate trust with this simple exercise: Give your child five dollars. Tell him or her that you will need that money to buy groceries later. Emphasize that you are trusting him or her to keep the money safe and give it to you when you need it. This is the same way we should trust God, believing that he will provide for us when we need something and not worrying about our future.*

Q: WHY DOESN'T GOD JUST GIVE US MONEY WHEN WE NEED IT?

21

A: God does give us money when we need it. God always meets our needs. But sometimes we don't see God's provision for what it is. God usually provides for us through jobs, people, and other ordinary means. Even though we don't think of these as "miracles," they still come from God.

God wants you to plan, to work, to be responsible, and to use well what he's already given to you. When you need something, God may want you to use something that you already have instead. Or he may want you to make something yourself instead of buying a new one. Or he may ask you to get along without whatever you think you need.

There is a difference between *need* and *want*. People often want a lot of things they don't really need. Your basic needs are a little bit of food, a few clothes, and someplace to sleep. Most of us have much, much more than we truly *need*.

You also should realize that God lets people experience the results of their own choices—including their choices about spending money. He doesn't rescue his people from every mistake they make. If you make lots of bad choices with your money, you will suffer lots of bad consequences.

KEY VERSES: *"My thoughts are completely different from yours," says the Lord. "And my ways are far beyond anything you could imagine. For just as the heavens are higher than the earth, so are my ways higher than your ways and my thoughts higher than your thoughts." (Isaiah 55:8-9)*

RELATED VERSES: *Psalm 138:7-8; 2 Thessalonians 3:10; Hebrews 13:5*

RELATED QUESTIONS: *Why do we work? How much money will God supply for us?*

22

A: People become rich for many different reasons. Some people are rich because they were born into rich families. Others become rich by working hard, saving, and investing wisely. A few get their money as gifts or by winning contests. Some people get their money illegally—they cheat others and commit crimes.

But some people who seem rich have lots of nice things but no money. They're so far in debt that they may never get out. They're not really rich; they just *look* that way.

Remember that "rich" and "poor" are just labels. Many people who live in poor countries would say that *everyone* in the United States is rich. They would say *you* are rich. Why? Because compared to them, you are. You have a lot more than they have.

You are truly rich only when you are content with what you have. If you have enough for your needs and enough to give some away, you can be content. Be glad just to love and serve God. Then you will be the richest person in town.

KEY VERSE: *[David prayed,] "Riches and honor come from you alone, for you rule over everything. Power and might are in your hand, and it is at your discretion that people are made great and given strength." (1 Chronicles 29:12)*

RELATED VERSES: *Deuteronomy 8:18; Proverbs 10:4, 22; 22:2; Ecclesiastes 5:19-20; 7:14; Ezekiel 28:5; Hosea 2:8*

RELATED QUESTIONS: *Why is everyone not equal? How do people get rich or poor? Why can't everybody be the same? How do rich people make so much money?*

Q: DO BILLIONAIRES STILL NEED TO TRUST GOD FOR MONEY THEY NEED?

23

A: *Everybody* needs to trust God for money, even billionaires. The Bible tells about a man named Job who lost all his wealth in one day. At the time, Job was one of the richest men alive.

No one has any money except what God lets them have. Billionaires get all their money from God, just as you do. God could take the money away in a second, just as he could give you a billion dollars in a second.

KEY VERSES: *This is what the Lord says: "Let not the wise man gloat in his wisdom, or the mighty man in his might, or the rich man in his riches. Let them boast in this alone: that they truly know me and understand that I am the Lord who is just and righteous, whose love is unfailing, and that I delight in these things. I, the Lord, have spoken!" (Jeremiah 9:23-24)*

RELATED VERSES: *Job 1:1–2:10; 42:12-17; Psalm 10; Proverbs 28:13; Ecclesiastes 5:10-12; Habakkuk 2:9; Matthew 6:19; 19:23-24*

RELATED QUESTION: *If you are not a Christian, will God still supply money for you?*

NOTE TO PARENTS: *If you talk or joke about wanting to be rich, your kids will get the impression that rich people are truly happier than the rest of us. But the reality is that rich people have more to worry about—much more (see Ecclesiastes 5:12). Remind your kids that every person should trust God for his or her needs, even billionaires. The key to happiness is loving God, not having more money.*

Q: WHY DOESN'T GOD TAKE RICH PEOPLE'S MONEY AND GIVE IT TO THE POOR PEOPLE?

24

A: God wants more than to just end poverty. He wants us to love each other as much as he loves us. Just imagine how awful it would be if everyone had plenty of money and no kindness. Money alone will not make anybody happy. But if everyone would obey God and love one another, we would be better people *and* happier.

That is why God has chosen to use his people to help others instead of just making everyone rich. He wants us to learn to be kind, generous, and wise. He wants people to love and help each other.

KEY VERSE: *Yes, you will be enriched so that you can give even more generously. And when we take your gifts to those who need them, they will break out in thanksgiving to God. (2 Corinthians 9:11)*

RELATED VERSES: *Ecclesiastes 5:8, 13; 6:1-2; Amos 4:1-2; Luke 12:33-34; Acts 20:33-35; 2 Corinthians 9:11-15*

RELATED QUESTIONS: *Why don't rich people give some money to the poor? Is God sometimes angry about our greed? How come God lets the poor be poor? Why does God let some people be rich and others poor?*

NOTE TO PARENTS: *It is important for children to understand that we are God's hands and feet in this world.*

Q: HOW DO POOR PEOPLE GET POOR?

25

A: Most people become poor by being born into poor families. In fact, many people in the world are born in a poor country where almost everyone is poor. It's not their fault that they are poor.

There are many other reasons for poverty too. Some people are born with a physical or mental handicap or they are injured in an accident or in war, and they find it very hard to get a good job. Some are poor because they have been cheated by other people. And some people become poor because they made bad choices.

No matter what makes someone poor, we must try to help. God is kind to us even though we make bad choices and mistakes. So we should be kind to others, even if we think it's their own fault that they are poor.

KEY VERSE: *A poor person's farm may produce much food, but injustice sweeps it all away. (Proverbs 13:23)*

RELATED VERSES: *Proverbs 22:2; 26:13-15; Ecclesiastes 7:14; Ezekiel 34:20-22; Amos 8:4-7; James 2:1-5*

RELATED QUESTIONS: *If poor people can read and do things, why can't they get a job? Why should we put money into the church for poor people when it's their fault they're poor? Why don't poor people get a job?*

NOTE TO PARENTS: *Never tell a child that poor people are always to blame for their own poverty, or that people always become poor because of wrongdoing. People become poor for many reasons, and misfortune and injustice are responsible for a lot of poverty (see Amos 8:4-7). Our duty as Christians is to help those who hurt.*

Q: WHY DOESN'T THE GOVERNMENT JUST PRINT MORE MONEY IN FACTORIES AND GIVE IT TO THE POOR?

26

A: Some governments have tried to print more money and give it to the poor. It did not work because very soon the money was worth very little.

Money is not just printed paper. It gets its value from something else. In our country, money gets its value from all the goods and services that people make. Each dollar means that someone somewhere did one dollar's worth of work. The more work we (the whole country) do, the more money we have. The less work we do, the less money we have.

The best way to help poor people get more money is to help them get jobs. That way they get paid while they also create more valuable goods and services.

KEY VERSE: *Hard workers have plenty of food; playing around brings poverty. (Proverbs 28:19)*

RELATED VERSES: *Proverbs 1:10-19; 20:21; 28:15, 22*

RELATED QUESTION: *Why can't we just get money without working?*

Q: WHY DIDN'T GOD GIVE US MONEY RIGHT AWAY WHEN MY DAD LOST HIS JOB?

27

A:

We don't always know why God does what he does. But we know that he loves us and has a plan for us, even for the hard times.

Sometimes God is working out something that we don't know about yet. Maybe it's even better than what we wanted or had before. God can use times like this to teach us to trust him more. As we trust him more, he can trust us with more.

Losing a job can be very painful and difficult. The person without a job wonders what he or she will do and where the money will come from. If your dad has lost his job, pitch in with any money you can. Say encouraging words to him. Donate your allowance. Do odd jobs for neighbors to earn more money if you can. Ask God to provide what you need, and trust him to do so.

KEY VERSE: *[God says,] "Trust me in your times of trouble, and I will rescue you, and you will give me glory." (Psalm 50:15)*

RELATED VERSES: *Psalm 138:7-8; Philippians 4:6-7, 19*

RELATED QUESTION: *Why doesn't God sometimes give money when you need it?*

NOTE TO PARENTS: *This question is difficult to answer when a family member has lost a job and needy dependents don't know what the future holds. But it is very important to avoid blaming God or anyone else. Pull together, help each other, and readjust your expectations of needs and wants. Take the experience as an opportunity to show your children what it means to live by faith.*

Q: WHY DOES GOD SOMETIMES WAIT UNTIL THE LAST MINUTE TO SUPPLY OUR NEEDS?

28

A: It may seem as though God waits until the last minute to supply your needs, but remember that God has a timetable that you can't see. He has a plan for you. Nothing can stop that plan, not even a shortage of money. God may wait because he wants you to trust him more. God always remembers you and hears your prayers. And he never runs out of anything.

Sometimes people wait till the last minute to pray. Instead, we should be praying to God all the time about our needs. We can trust him to take care of us.

KEY VERSES: *[Moses said,] "For forty years I led you through the wilderness, yet your clothes and sandals did not wear out. You had no bread or wine or other strong drink, but he gave you food so you would know that he is the Lord your God." (Deuteronomy 29:5-6)*

RELATED VERSES: *Psalm 138:7-8*

RELATED QUESTION: *How do you trust God when things are going rough?*

NOTE TO PARENTS: *This question can arise when a child hears about God providing for someone in the nick of time, such as right before a rent check is due. Remind your family that God provides for us day after day. Moses pointed out to the Israelites that God had prevented their sandals and clothes from wearing out for forty years (Deuteronomy 29:5). Just like the Israelites, we sometimes forget that God is providing for us all the time. Thank God for all he has given so far.*

Q: IF GOD OWNS EVERYTHING, WHY DOESN'T HE KEEP IT ALL IN HEAVEN?

29

A: God owns everything because he is the Lord of all. But he created all good things for *us* to use and enjoy. He didn't create things just so he could keep them all or even because he needed them. He mainly wants *us* to use them and to use them wisely so we will be happy.

Remember that God is spirit. He doesn't need money, toys, food, or other things. What would he do with all our stuff? He would rather give it to us so we can learn to be responsible and use it in his service.

KEY VERSES: *[God says,] "For all the animals of the forest are mine, and I own the cattle on a thousand hills. Every bird of the mountains and all the animals of the field belong to me." (Psalm 50:10-11)*

RELATED VERSES: *Job 41:11; Acts 17:28; 1 Timothy 6:17*

RELATED QUESTIONS: *If God owns everything, why do we have to make money? Why are the things you buy God's?*

NOTE TO PARENTS: *Always tie ownership of things to stewardship of those things. Having a pet means feeding and taking care of it. Having a toy means using it properly and putting it away when you're done. Reward your children whenever they show good stewardship by being more willing to grant their next request. And be sure to say why you're so willing.*

Q: IF GOD OWNS EVERYTHING, WHY DO PEOPLE SELL STUFF LIKE IT IS THEIR OWN AND CHARGE HOWEVER MUCH THEY WANT FOR IT?

30

A: God owns everything because he created everything and is in charge of everything. But God trusts people with things and money. He makes people managers of the things they have. God has given you your toys, for example. Those toys are yours to take care of. As part of that responsibility, you may decide one day that you are too old for them and want to sell them or give them away. If your parents say it's OK, you can sell those things and use the money for other things. Just remember to set fair prices.

KEY VERSE: *[David prayed,] "Who am I, and who are my people, that we could give anything to you? Everything we have has come from you, and we give you only what you have already given us!" (1 Chronicles 29:14)*

RELATED VERSES: *Leviticus 25:17, 23; Nehemiah 5:1-7; Job 41:11; Psalm 8:6; Proverbs 11:26; Acts 4:36-37*

RELATED QUESTIONS: *If God owns everything, then why do we have to pay for things? What is stewardship?*

NOTE TO PARENTS: *Helping your children clean up and sell old things and then allowing them to use that money to buy something they want can teach them a lot about the benefit of taking care of the things they manage.*

Q: WHY DID JESUS TALK ABOUT MONEY WHEN HE DIDN'T HAVE VERY MUCH?

31

A: We don't know how much money Jesus had. We know that he didn't own a home and that he had few possessions. But we also know that he had everything he needed. The Bible doesn't say that Jesus or the disciples lived in poverty. Luke 8:3 tells us that the wives of some wealthy men gave money to support Jesus and his disciples. Judas was in charge of the money bag.

Jesus talked about money because he wanted to teach us how to use it right. He knew that we would love money and be tempted to be greedy. And he knew that the love of money leads to all kinds of evil. How we feel about money and how we use it matter a great deal.

KEY VERSES: *Among them were Mary Magdalene, from whom he had cast out seven demons; Joanna, the wife of Chuza, Herod's business manager; Susanna; and many others who were contributing from their own resources to support Jesus and his disciples. (Luke 8:2-3)*

RELATED VERSES: *Luke 9:58; 22:35-36*

RELATED QUESTIONS: *Why did Jesus talk so much about money? Why would Jesus talk about money?*

NOTE TO PARENTS: *Be careful not to idealize poverty or imply that being like Jesus means going hungry. If you sense that your child is afraid of being poor "like Jesus," reassure him or her that Jesus was not poverty-stricken. He had everything he needed. God met all his needs, and God will meet ours, too.*

Q: DID JESUS EVER HAVE PROBLEMS WITH MONEY?

32

A: If you mean "Did Jesus have trouble paying his bills?" the answer is no. God provided all Jesus needed. Jesus never lived in poverty. People gave money to him and to the disciples so they could spend most of their time telling people about God's good news. Jesus had enough money for all his bills.

If you mean "Did Jesus ever spend money foolishly?" again the answer is no. Judas once accused Jesus of misusing money, but the truth was that Judas had been stealing from Jesus (John 12:1-6).

KEY VERSES: *Jesus said, ". . . Open the mouth of the first fish you catch, and you will find a coin. Take the coin and pay the tax for both of us." (Matthew 17:26-27)*

RELATED VERSE: *Luke 8:3*

RELATED QUESTIONS: *Did Jesus rely on money? Did Jesus spend his money wisely or foolishly? Did Jesus like money?*

NOTE TO PARENTS: *A question like this naturally follows a child's struggle to understand exactly how Jesus was human. Make a distinction between needing money, which Jesus did—and mishandling money, which Jesus didn't. Taxes are a good example. Jesus had to pay them just like everyone else. He did not try to avoid his duty to pay taxes or squander his money and become unable to pay them.*

Q: IS MONEY ONE OF THE MOST IMPORTANT THINGS IN LIFE?

33

A: Money is both very important and not at all important. Money makes it possible for us to pay bills and buy food and other things we need. Money also helps us support God's work in the world. We can use money to help feed hungry people, clothe poor people, and share the good news about Jesus with people all over the world. We need money to do these things.

Money is not the *most* important thing in life, however. The most important thing in life is our relationship with God. Only God can forgive our sins, and only God can teach us how to live. The people God has put in our lives are also much more important than money. Money can't buy you a new mom or dad, good friends, good health, or good neighbors. Money can't buy you any of the things that matter most in life.

So put God at the top of your list. Then put your family and friends. Then put everyone else God created. And then put money underneath all of those. Use money to serve people, not the other way around.

KEY VERSES: *Being wise is as good as being rich; in fact, it is better. Wisdom or money can get you almost anything, but it's important to know that only wisdom can save your life. (Ecclesiastes 7:11-12)*

RELATED VERSES: *Matthew 6:19-34; Luke 12:13-21; John 12:6*

RELATED QUESTIONS: *Why do people try to get money? Why is money so important?*

Q: IF SALVATION IS FREE, WHY DO WE HAVE TO BUY A BIBLE?

34

A: We pay for Bibles because it costs money to produce them. The publishers that publish them, the printers that print them, and the stores that sell them all need to be able to pay their workers. God tells us to pay what we owe (Leviticus 19:13), and the price we pay for a Bible pays the workers' wages.

The Bible is God's Word. It's reasonable to pay for something so important.

Salvation, on the other hand, comes from God and *is* free, but it has nothing to do with money. God says that the penalty for sin is death. If you sin, you must die. That means that you will be separated from God forever. God sent his only Son, Jesus, to die on the cross in our place. Because Jesus did not sin, he did not have to die. But he chose to die in our place. If we ask God to forgive our sins and accept that Jesus died in our place, God will forgive us. We will become his children. So salvation is *free* for us because we do not have to pay the penalty for our sins. Jesus paid it.

KEY VERSES: *For if you confess with your mouth that Jesus is Lord and believe in your heart that God raised him from the dead, you will be saved. For it is by believing in your heart that you are made right with God, and it is by confessing with your mouth that you are saved. (Romans 10:9-10)*

RELATED VERSES: *Romans 3:23-26; 5:8; 6:23; 2 Corinthians 5:15*

LIVING
AND
GIVING

Q: WHAT IS TITHING?

35

A: *Tithe* is a word used in the Bible. It means "a tenth." In Old Testament times, God commanded the Israelites to give to the priests a tithe of all they produced. They gave sheep, grain, cows, and so forth. These tithes were like income for the priests, enabling them to work full-time leading the people in worship and taking care of God's house. Sometimes people gave even more to say thank you to God for all the good things he had provided. Their giving showed that they trusted God to supply their needs.

Many Christians use the word *tithe* to describe the giving they do. Usually they mean that they give back to God a portion of their income. Sometimes they give a tenth (10 percent); sometimes they give less or more. When we give gladly, we show that we trust God to take care of us.

KEY VERSE: *[God said,] "Should people cheat God? Yet you have cheated me! But you ask, 'What do you mean? When did we ever cheat you?' You have cheated me of the tithes and offerings due to me." (Malachi 3:8)*

RELATED VERSES: *Leviticus 27:30-33; Deuteronomy 14:22-29; 2 Chronicles 31:5-6; 1 Corinthians 16:1-2*

RELATED QUESTION: *How much are you supposed to tithe?*

NOTE TO PARENTS: *Some parents require that their kids tithe; they want their children to develop this important habit early in life. Other parents are reluctant to require it; they want their children to give willingly. One way to handle this is to require your children to give, tell them about tithing and what you do, but let them decide how much they want to give. Whatever the amount, help them set aside a portion for God every time they earn money.*

Q: WHY DO I HAVE TO GIVE MONEY TO CHURCH?

36

A: It is part of God's plan for Christians to give money to the church so the church can do God's work and help others learn how to follow him. Like families and businesses, churches have bills to pay—electric bills, phone bills, water bills, and many other expenses. Churches also have to pay salaries to the pastors and secretaries. The church's money pays for ministries such as Sunday school, missions, and special events. Churches don't sell tickets for the worship services or sell products, so they get their money from people in the congregation who give freely.

God's people have always given money to those who lead in worship and service to God. Abraham did it. The Israelites did it. Jesus did it. The apostles did it. Everyone who loves God does it. They know it is a lot of work to lead God's people, so they pitch in and help pay for it.

KEY VERSE: *For I can testify that they gave not only what they could afford but far more. And they did it of their own free will. (2 Corinthians 8:3)*

RELATED VERSES: *Proverbs 27:10; Luke 6:38; 2 Corinthians 5:11; 8:2-15; 9:12-14; Galatians 6:6; 1 Timothy 5:17*

RELATED QUESTION: *Did God or Jesus say that we have to give money to the church, or do we just do it?*

NOTE TO PARENTS: *Help your kids understand that the church is a community. It is a group of people who all share a relationship with Christ, much like a family. And like a family, every person should pitch in and help make it work.*

Q: HOW MUCH SHOULD A PERSON GIVE TO THE CHURCH?

A: Christians are free to give as much as they want to the church. But many like to start with 10 percent of their income. That's their tithe. Those who are able should give even more to other people and ministries that serve God.

Just be careful not to brag about your giving. Jesus scolded the Pharisees for boasting about what they gave (Matthew 23:23). He said, "When you give to someone, don't tell your left hand what your right hand is doing. Give your gifts in secret, and your Father, who knows all secrets, will reward you" (Matthew 6:3-4).

Some people need to ask a different question: Why am I not giving anything to the church? Some people can't bring themselves to give 10 percent but start smaller and pray that God will help them increase their giving. It's better to give *something* than to wait until you have enough to give a lot.

KEY VERSE: *You must each make up your own mind as to how much you should give. Don't give reluctantly or in response to pressure. For God loves the person who gives cheerfully. (2 Corinthians 9:7)*

RELATED VERSES: *Matthew 6:1-4; Mark 12:41-44; Luke 6:38; Acts 20:33-35; 2 Corinthians 8:11*

NOTE TO PARENTS: *Children can be very generous givers. They will often give money to people whom they like just to show their affection or give everything they have on a wave of good feeling. If your child wants to give extra, talk about it. Ask whether the gift matches the need. Explore other ways of giving besides handing over cash. You don't need to protect them from every mistake—they'll learn from the experience—but you can give them guidance.*

Q: WHY DO SOME PEOPLE KEEP ALL THEIR MONEY TO THEMSELVES INSTEAD OF GIVING SOME TO GOD?

38

A: It is true that some people do not give any money to the church. Some of them haven't learned to trust God yet—they are afraid to let go of their money. They are growing in their faith and are just learning to trust him. Some don't know that they have a responsibility to give. Some are just greedy. If you know of someone like this, pray that they will learn to trust in God instead of their money.

But be careful not to spy on others and try to figure out who is a good giver and who isn't. You can never really know how much people give or whether it's a little or a lot in God's sight. Jesus once told about a poor widow who gave only two small coins (Mark 12:41-44). Jesus said she gave more than the rich people did because she gave all she had. Set a good example yourself and let God teach everyone else how to give.

KEY VERSE: *If you are really eager to give, it isn't important how much you are able to give. God wants you to give what you have, not what you don't have. (2 Corinthians 8:12)*

RELATED VERSES: *1 Samuel 8:3; Luke 12:15-21; Ephesians 5:5; 1 Timothy 6:6-10; James 4:2-3*

RELATED QUESTION: *If you're saving up for something, is it OK not to give some money to the church?*

NOTE TO PARENTS: *This question gives you a good opportunity to expand your child's idea of giving to include other kinds of selflessness. Whenever your child shares a toy, defers to someone else's choice of video, or lets someone else get the bigger dessert, affirm your child for giving.*

Q: WHERE DOES THE MONEY I GIVE TO CHURCH GO?

39

A: It goes to the church's bank account, where it stays until the church treasurer writes checks to pay all the church's expenses. The church has to pay for the building, heat, light, phone, postage, Sunday school supplies, pastors' salaries, staff salaries, missions, and other ministries and expenses.

A gift to God's people is a gift to God. Give because you are thankful for all God has given you, and he will take care of you.

KEY VERSES: *Don't you know that those who work in the Temple get their meals from the food brought to the Temple as offerings? And those who serve at the altar get a share of the sacrificial offerings. In the same way, the Lord gave orders that those who preach the Good News should be supported by those who benefit from it. (1 Corinthians 9:13-14)*

RELATED VERSES: *Psalm 40:6-8; 51:16-19; Jeremiah 7:21-23; Micah 6:6-8; Malachi 3:8-12*

RELATED QUESTION: *When you give money to the church, what do they use it for?*

NOTE TO PARENTS: *Most kids never see where their offerings go or what becomes of them. It's OK for them to wonder. Explain as much as you can how your church uses its money. Name programs that your kids know, point to staff who receive salaries from the church, and mention missionaries they've heard of before.*

Q: HOW DOES GOD GET THE MONEY THAT I GIVE TO HIM?

40

A: When people say that they are giving money to God, they mean that they are giving it to the church, to a missionary, to the poor, or to other people *in service to God.* In other words, they give money *to* people *in obedience to* God or *in God's name.* And they are giving it for a specific purpose: to help God's people. You don't give money directly to God. He doesn't reach down with a hand and take it from you or from a special spot where you put it. Instead, you give money to people in God's name and for God's work.

This is exactly the way God wants it. We show our love for God by loving others (1 John 2:9-11; 4:20-21).

KEY VERSES: *Then these righteous ones will reply, "Lord, when did we ever see you hungry and feed you? Or thirsty and give you something to drink? Or a stranger and show you hospitality? Or naked and give you clothing? When did we ever see you sick or in prison, and visit you?" And the King will tell them, "I assure you, when you did it to one of the least of these my brothers and sisters, you were doing it to me!" (Matthew 25:37-40)*

RELATED VERSES: *Proverbs 19:17; Matthew 25:31-46; 1 Timothy 5:17-18; 1 John 2:9-11*

RELATED QUESTIONS: *Sometimes it seems like God doesn't provide for the poor people. Why? Is it because we are supposed to help them?*

NOTE TO PARENTS: *Take a question like this as an opportunity to explain the different ways giving supports God's work—through church, through other ministries, and in other countries.*

Q: DO WE HAVE TO GIVE MONEY TO POOR PEOPLE?

41

A: Christians have the responsibility to help people who have needs, including poor people. One reason for this is that God cares about people in need, and we should all try to be like God.

You can help the poor in many ways. For example, you can give food to a community food pantry or soup kitchen, serve meals at a rescue mission, give money to programs that help poor children, or give money to organizations that help the poor.

Remember, everything you have came from God's goodness and kindness to you. He wants you to treat others the way he treats you.

KEY VERSE: *If any of your Israelite relatives fall into poverty and cannot support themselves, support them as you would a resident foreigner and allow them to live with you. (Leviticus 25:35)*

RELATED VERSES: *Leviticus 25:35-38; Deuteronomy 15:7-11; Psalm 82:3; Proverbs 14:20-21; 22:9; 31:8-9; Ezekiel 18:7-8, 12-13, 16-17; Luke 12:33-34; Acts 20:33-35; 2 Corinthians 8:9; 9:12*

RELATED QUESTION: *Should we give poor people money because it's nice?*

NOTE TO PARENTS: *This can be a difficult issue for kids because they lack the discernment to judge the merits of every giving opportunity. Fear of strangers, a sense of fairness, and knowledge that Christians should give all point them in different directions. Try to do some charitable giving as a family so you can provide guided practice.*

Q: IS IT WRONG TO SEE POOR PEOPLE ON THE STREET AND NOT GIVE THEM ANY MONEY?

42

A: No. God doesn't expect you to give money to *everyone* who asks. If you did, you would soon run out of money entirely. But it would also be wrong to never give anybody anything.

There are many poor people who desperately need money, food, and clothes. It is good that you feel compassion for them and want to give. But you can help them in many ways besides just giving money. You can also give to food pantries, support international organizations that serve in very poor countries, or give clothing and other good used things to places in your community that help the poor.

Not everyone who asks for money really needs your help. Some pretend to be poor to get money. Some are lazy and beg instead of going to work. You have to use good judgment. Your parents can help you know when to give, and you can pray for wisdom. It is best to give to people you know and whose needs you know to be real.

KEY VERSES: *If there are any poor people in your towns when you arrive in the land the Lord your God is giving you, do not be hard-hearted or tightfisted toward them. Instead, be generous and lend them whatever they need. (Deuteronomy 15:7-8)*

RELATED VERSES: *Leviticus 25:35-38; Deuteronomy 15:7-11; Proverbs 11:24; 14:20-21; 21:13; 22:9; 28:27; 31:8-9; Luke 6:38; 10:25-37; 12:33-34; Acts 20:33-35*

RELATED QUESTIONS: *When we give money to poor people, how do we know if they will use it for clothes or food? Should you give money to poor people if they spend it on drugs?*

Q:

WHERE DOES ALL THE MONEY FROM FOUNTAINS AND WISHING WELLS GO?

WISHING WELL

RIVER BANK

43

A: Some people think that if they wish for something when they throw a coin into a fountain or a wishing well, they'll get their wish. That's just not true. It's superstition. Fountains and magic don't control anything—God does.

The good news is that many people who have fountains and wishing wells on their property collect the money and give it to charities. That's a good way to use the money.

It's fun to throw change into a fountain or a wishing well. But if you do, don't bother to make a wish. Instead, pray for the people who will benefit from the money.

KEY VERSE: *Many sorrows come to the wicked, but unfailing love surrounds those who trust the Lord. (Psalm 32:10)*

RELATED VERSES: *Psalm 4:5; 37:3; 125:1; 131:3; Isaiah 26:4*

RELATED QUESTIONS: *Is it wrong to throw money down a well and wish? What do the malls and parks do with the money from the public money fountains?*

NOTE TO PARENTS: *If you allow your children to throw money into fountains, remind them that it's just a game. Don't propagate the superstition that their wish will get some power from their throwing money into the water. God is Lord of all (Psalm 33:18-19).*

A PENNY SAVED

Q: WHAT IS THE REASON FOR LEARNING TO SAVE MONEY?

Jason for President in 2044

44

A:
It is important to save money because you will need the money in the future for things that you don't need now. For example, you may want to buy something that costs a lot, you may want to buy a special gift for a friend, you may have an emergency and need money quickly, or you may want to go to college. People who don't save for these things have to borrow money to pay for them. But then they have to pay back the loan *plus* interest. It's better to save up for what you will need so that when you need the money it's there.

KEY VERSES: *Take a lesson from the ants, you lazybones. Learn from their ways and be wise! Even though they have no prince, governor, or ruler to make them work, they labor hard all summer, gathering food for the winter. (Proverbs 6:6-8)*

RELATED VERSES: *Genesis 41:35-36; Proverbs 10:5; 13:11; 14:4; 20:4; 22:3; 1 Timothy 5:8*

RELATED QUESTION: *What if I don't have enough money to support myself when I'm older?*

NOTE TO PARENTS: *Help your kids divide the money they get into three parts: some to give to the Lord, some for savings, and some to spend. (One possible plan would be 10 percent giving, 40 percent saving, and 50 percent spending.) This way they are not frustrated by saving because they have some immediate spending money. Then help them set a short-term goal for saving. Make sure it's something they really want. This will help them begin to realize the power to purchase the things they want because they have saved for them.*

Q: WHAT SHOULD WE KNOW ABOUT SAVING MONEY?

45

A: Here are seven important facts about saving money:

1. God wants us to do it because he knows we need to.

2. It's important because it's part of God's plan for meeting our needs.

3. It's difficult now but will reward us later.

4. It takes planning and work but less effort than getting out of debt.

5. Responsible people do it because they know they will need it someday.

6. It should be done for a specific purpose, so you know when to use the money you have saved.

7. Most people are not good at it.

Try to have a purpose for all your saving. It will be easier to set aside some money each week if you have a goal in mind. For example, you may want to save for a special trip or for college.

KEY VERSE: *The wise have wealth and luxury, but fools spend whatever they get. (Proverbs 21:20)*

RELATED VERSES: *Genesis 41:35-36; Deuteronomy 8:11; Proverbs 6:8; 10:5; 13:11; 14:4; 20:4; 22:3; 1 Timothy 5:8; James 5:1-6*

RELATED QUESTION: *Why do we need money at all?*

NOTE TO PARENTS: *If your child doesn't appreciate the reasons for saving money, give him or her some practice. Start small and work up to more challenging goals. First have your child save up for something that costs only two allowances. As time goes by, set bigger goals. Eventually your child will build a habit of purposeful saving.*

Q: WHAT IS THE QUICKEST WAY TO SAVE MONEY?

46

A: The easiest and quickest way to save money is to set some aside *every time* you get some. You may want to begin by putting some in a jar. Then when you get a few dollars, you can put it in the bank.

Some people don't save because they think they can't save enough to make it worthwhile. But it may surprise you how much you end up saving when you save a little out of every bit that comes in.

Remember these things about saving:

Have a *purpose* for your saving and write it down. Example: "I want to buy _____."

- Have a *plan*. Example: "I will set aside half of my allowance and any other money I get."
- Have a *procedure*. Example: "Put the cash in a jar every week and take it to the bank once a month." Or "Write down new total each time I put in some money."

KEY VERSE: *Those who love pleasure become poor; wine and luxury are not the way to riches. (Proverbs 21:17)*

RELATED VERSES: *Proverbs 13:11; 16:8; 19:1; 20:21, 23; 21:6, 20; 22:3*

RELATED QUESTION: *Are savings bonds good for saving money?*

NOTE TO PARENTS: *Whenever your child wants to save up for something, ask him or her to describe the purpose, plan, and procedure for the project. (If you have preschoolers or early grade-school kids, use the words* why, when, *and* how.) *Write down the goal with the amount that's needed and put it with his or her savings where it will serve as a reminder.*

Q: IF I PUT MONEY IN A SAVINGS ACCOUNT, CAN I GET IT BACK?

47

A: Oh, yes! The bank is just a holding place for your money. It's like a big piggy bank. Later, when you need it, you will be able to get your money back. To get money from your savings account, just go to the bank with Mom or Dad and fill out a withdrawal slip. The teller will give you the money, and the computer will keep track of how much you took out. The money is yours, and you can always get it.

Remember, the purpose of a savings account is to save for the future. Try not to take money out until you've reached your goal.

Do not get too attached to your money, though. God doesn't want us to trust in our savings. He wants us to trust in *him*. God will help you save, and he will take care of you no matter what. Remember that God—not money, banks, or anything else here on earth—is your provider. Place your trust in God.

KEY VERSE: *If your wealth increases, don't make it the center of your life. (Psalm 62:10)*

RELATED VERSES: *Jeremiah 22:17; Matthew 25:26-27; James 5:1-6*

NOTE TO PARENTS: *The first time your child opens a savings account, you might want to go back to the bank together after a few days and take some money out just for practice. Also, once he or she has set a savings goal, help your child stick to it.*

Q: IS IT SELFISH TO SAVE MONEY?

PIGGY BANKS FOR SALE

48

A: Saving money *can* be selfish, but it doesn't have to be. We need to plan ahead and save for future needs, so we need to save. If we don't, we are being foolish. But we also need to give. We need to trust God to meet our needs. If we try to save *all* our money and never share any of it, we aren't trusting God, we're trusting in our money. That's called hoarding, and God doesn't like it. Saving should always meet a future need. It should not just make us richer.

Most selfish people show their selfishness by spending all their money on themselves, not by saving it.

KEY VERSE: *Don't be selfish; don't live to make a good impression on others. Be humble, thinking of others as better than yourself. (Philippians 2:3)*

RELATED VERSES: *Deuteronomy 8:11; Proverbs 21:20; Luke 12:13-21; James 4:1-3; 5:1-6*

RELATED QUESTIONS: *Is it better for people to save their money? Does Jesus want us to spend money?*

NOTE TO PARENTS: *Emphasize that saving is good if it is for a good purpose, such as providing for some future need. It is bad if it's just for hoarding. Help your child set goals for saving. Don't let him or her continue to save without a goal.*

Q: WHY DO SOME PEOPLE HIDE THEIR MONEY?

49

A: Most people who hide money do so because they don't want their money to be stolen. The world has many bad people who look for ways to take other people's money. So people on a trip may hide their money in their motel room or suitcase. And just about everyone keeps some money in their wallet or purse when they walk around town. A good steward is careful with his or her money.

People who hide large amounts of money usually don't trust the banks. They think their money will be safer if they hide it in their house or in the ground. But we should not be so afraid that we bury our money. God will take care of us even if something happens to our money.

Some people even hide money because they got it illegally. They know that if someone finds them with it, they will get in trouble. But in the end they will be found out anyway. They can't run from God forever.

KEY VERSES: *The servant with the one bag of gold came and said, "Sir, I know you are a hard man, harvesting crops you didn't plant and gathering crops you didn't cultivate. I was afraid I would lose your money, so I hid it in the earth and here it is." (Matthew 25:24-25)*

RELATED VERSES: *Genesis 32:7-8; Matthew 6:19; 25:18, 26-27*

RELATED QUESTION: *How come some older people spend all their money and don't put money in savings bonds each time they get paid?*

NOTE TO PARENTS: *Explain to your child that hiding small amounts of money is fine, but large amounts should be placed in the bank. It is a safer place to keep money, and the money will earn interest.*

Q: IS THE STOCK MARKET A PLACE WHERE YOU BUY ANIMALS?

50

A: Sometimes animals are called "stock" or "live-stock" by people who raise them. But the stock market is a place where people trade companies, not animals. Anyone who buys stock in a company becomes part owner of that company. They can sell their stock to other people if they want to. Meanwhile, the company gets to spend the money on supplies, equipment, and workers that help the company grow.

Buying stock is one way to save for the future. The shares of a company are worth money. If a company does well, its stock price will go up. People who own the stock can sell it at the higher price. But if the company does not do well, the price will go down. People who sell their stock at the lower price will lose money. That's why it's unwise to put all your savings in stock.

KEY VERSE: *The servant who received the five bags of gold began immediately to invest the money and soon doubled it. (Matthew 25:16)*

RELATED VERSE: *Genesis 34:21*

RELATED QUESTION: *How do you make investments—where do you go?*

NOTE TO PARENTS: *If you invest in the stock market, show your children what you are doing and how you do it. Let them see the results as well. If they are really interested, let them buy a small part of your share. Then when you sell or when they want to sell, return their money plus their earnings or minus their losses. (Don't shelter them from losses. They need to learn both sides.)*

Q: HOW CAN RETIRED PEOPLE GO ON TRIPS IF THEY DON'T HAVE A JOB?

51

A: Retired people can go on vacation trips because they saved their money when they were working. They put some in the bank and probably invested some more. And they started when they were young, like you.

In order to go on trips when you don't have a job, you have to save up for a long time. You have to start when you're young. That is why saving is so important. One day, you too will want to retire.

KEY VERSES: *The Lord also instructed Moses, "This is the rule the Levites must follow: They must begin serving in the Tabernacle at the age of twenty-five, and they must retire at the age of fifty." (Numbers 8:23-25)*

RELATED VERSES: *1 Samuel 8:1; 1 Chronicles 29:26-28*

RELATED QUESTION: *What should you do if you're retired and you go on a trip and come back and find out the retirement plan is gone?*

NOTE TO PARENTS: *This is a good time to have a live example of the benefits of saving. Ask your retired relatives to tell your child how they saved for retirement. You could even illustrate this way: If you invest fifty cents every week at 8 percent interest, starting when you're 8 years old, you would have $25,798.86 (before taxes) by the time you're 65.*

Q: HOW MUCH DO INVESTMENTS COST?

52

A: An investment is something you buy so you can sell it later at a higher price. Investments, like stocks, have all different prices. Some cost more than others. Most investments cost more than children can pay. That's why most kids have their money in bank savings accounts, not in stocks or other investments like that.

Some people say you can get rich quickly or easily by buying their investment. The Bible warns us to stay away from those kinds of tricks. God's plan is that we trust him and that we let our money grow bit by bit. Greed causes us to listen to get-rich-quick ideas because we want more quickly. But trying to do it this way usually results in a loss, not a gain.

KEY VERSE: *Don't begin until you count the cost. For who would begin construction of a building without first getting estimates and then checking to see if there is enough money to pay the bills? (Luke 14:28)*

RELATED VERSES: *Matthew 25:14-30; Luke 12:15*

RELATED QUESTION: *What is an investment?*

NOTE TO PARENTS: *This topic is only hypothetical to kids who have no investments in the traditional sense, but it is a good way to talk about value. An investment pays you something back. The most expensive investment is one that never pays anything. The next time your child wants to buy something, encourage him or her to ask, "What am I getting for my money?"*

GOTTA
HAVE IT

Q: WHY DO PARENTS SOMETIMES NOT LET KIDS BUY WHAT WE WANT, EVEN WHEN WE HAVE ENOUGH MONEY FOR IT?

53

A: Usually parents stop their children from buying everything they want because they love their children.

Sometimes you want something that isn't good for you. Your parents know this and forbid it. When you were a baby, you may have wanted to drink drain cleaner because the bottle was colorful. You didn't know any better, and you thought it would be good. Your parents stopped you because they knew the drain cleaner would hurt you.

Your parents also want you to learn discipline so you can control your desires. You can't buy *everything*, because if you did, you would soon run out of money.

You can buy a lot of things with your money, but that doesn't mean you should buy all of them. You have to make choices—to buy some things and not others. Your parents are trying to help you learn these skills.

KEY VERSE: *Only a fool despises a parent's discipline; whoever learns from correction is wise. (Proverbs 15:5)*

RELATED VERSES: *Proverbs 13:1; 21:17, 20; Luke 12:15; Galatians 5:22-23; Ephesians 6:1; Colossians 3:20*

RELATED QUESTION: *If I get my own money, how come my parents say I can't buy certain things?*

NOTE TO PARENTS: *Strike a balance between boundaries and freedom. Let your children spend their spending money however they want to. Let them set their own saving goals. Then establish the rule that if it's their idea, they pay, and if it's your idea, you pay. This gives them enough control to buy what they want but restrains them to using their money, not yours. And it really cuts down on the "gimmes."*

Q: WHY CAN'T I HAVE ALL THE THINGS I WANT?

54

A: There are at least three reasons: First, you don't ask God for them. Second, you ask God for them, but you want them only for yourself, so he says no. Third, they cost too much or are bad for you, so your parents say no. God wants you to love him, help others, give to his work, and be content. Money gets in the way of all that. You can't spend all day, every day shopping and also love God, help others, give to his work, and be content. Sooner or later you have to stop being selfish.

You don't need all the things you want anyway. And think about this: If you got everything you wanted, what would you do with all that stuff?

KEY VERSE: *Then [Jesus] said, "Beware! Don't be greedy for what you don't have. Real life is not measured by how much we own." (Luke 12:15)*

RELATED VERSES: *Proverbs 21:17; Ecclesiastes 5:10-12; 6:9; James 4:1-3; 1 John 2:15-17*

RELATED QUESTIONS: *Why don't my parents buy expensive things for me, only clothes? Why do parents not buy us a lot of things? How come when you want something and you're going to pay, your parents won't let you have it?*

NOTE TO PARENTS: *Most kids pressure parents to buy things they want. Do not let your kids nag you into buying things. They will survive without them. Don't let kids convince you that they can't be happy without that special something. What people want most—a loving family and loyal friends—can never be bought. Learning to do without is one of the most powerful skills you can teach your children.*

Q: WHY DO PEOPLE FIGHT OVER MONEY?

55

A: One reason is greed. Some people want more money than they have, and they want it so much that they fight to get it. They are being selfish.

Another reason is that families just have to work out an agreement. Sometimes families argue about money because husbands and wives need to agree on how they are going to manage and spend their money. They should not fight about it, but it does take time to work out a plan, and they may not agree at first.

Always remember that people are more important than money. Talk over your money problems rather than fight about them. But if you can't agree, it's usually better to let someone else have his or her way than to lose a friend because of a fight over money.

KEY VERSE: *Greed causes fighting; trusting the Lord leads to prosperity. (Proverbs 28:25)*

RELATED VERSES: *Ecclesiastes 6:9; Luke 12:13-21; James 4:1-3; 1 John 2:15-17*

RELATED QUESTIONS: *Why do parents, when they go out with a friend for lunch, always argue about who is paying? Why do people argue about money? Why does money make people mad?*

NOTE TO PARENTS: *This question highlights the importance of contentment. People fight over money because they want what they don't have. Whenever a question like this comes up, remind your child that it's better to be content than to have more money.*

Q: WHY DO PEOPLE WANT MORE MONEY IF THEY ALREADY HAVE LOTS OF IT?

56

A: Greed makes people want more and more and more. They feel as if they never have enough, even though they really do. Greedy people become so worried about money that they think about it all the time. Greedy people are never satisfied, never content. God wants us to be satisfied and to find our contentment in him.

Sometimes people want more money for good reasons. They want to do something for God's kingdom or for other people, such as giving to those who have lost their homes or spreading the message of Jesus.

KEY VERSE: *Those who love money will never have enough. How absurd to think that wealth brings true happiness! (Ecclesiastes 5:10)*

RELATED VERSES: *Proverbs 27:20; Ecclesiastes 5:10-12; Ezekiel 33:31; Luke 12:13-21; Philippians 4:11-12; Hebrews 13:5; 1 John 2:15-17*

RELATED QUESTIONS: *Why do rich people have so much money? If people have lots of money, why do they rob?*

NOTE TO PARENTS: *A question like this may arise when news of professional athletes' contract negotiations hits the front page. It's a fair question, one that occurs to many adults as well as kids. Rather than condemn rich people, use the opportunity to point out that an addiction to money hurts. Greed and selfishness are terrible forces in a person's life, making otherwise nice people act cruel, unfair, and even criminal.*

Q: IS BUYING A LOTTERY TICKET THE SAME AS GAMBLING?

57

A: Yes. Gambling is when you buy a chance to win a big amount of money with a small amount of money, so buying a lottery ticket is the same as gambling.

The difference between gambling and investing is that in investing you are buying a product—a piece of a company or a bond, for example. In gambling, you are just buying a "chance." And your chances of winning are very poor. In fact, the only way you can win is if a lot of other people lose. That's not a good or wise way to use money.

It's fun to play games and it's fun to win a prize, but don't let it turn into gambling. A game becomes gambling when you try to win a large amount with a small amount. Your whole reason should be to have fun, not to get rich.

_____

KEY VERSE: *Yes, a person is a fool to store up earthly wealth but not have a rich relationship with God. (Luke 12:21)*

RELATED VERSES: *1 Timothy 6:9-10*

RELATED QUESTIONS: *Is it wrong to buy a lottery ticket hoping to get money out of it? Where does the lottery money that people win come from?*

Q: WHY DO PEOPLE PLAY THE LOTTERY IF THEY PROBABLY WON'T WIN?

58

A: People gamble and play the lottery because they *hope* to win. They imagine winning, and they imagine how much it would enable them to buy. They think that having a lot of money would solve all their problems. Meanwhile, the cost of one lottery ticket is very low, so people figure they aren't losing much.

Playing the lottery is a foolish thing to do. It plays right into our love of money, which Jesus warned us against. Many people who win millions in lotteries end up worse off than they were before. They spend all the money and have more problems than ever. That's because having lots of money doesn't solve your money problems. You need only to manage your money according to God's principles to have enough.

Being rich and having more can actually make your life worse. You have a lot more to manage and a lot more to lose. Loving God and others and receiving their love in return are the keys to happiness, not more things or more money.

KEY VERSE: *Wealth from get-rich-quick schemes quickly disappears; wealth from hard work grows. (Proverbs 13:11)*

RELATED VERSES: *1 Samuel 8:3; Proverbs 28:20, 22; Luke 11:39; 12:13-21*

RELATED QUESTIONS: *Why do people buy lottery tickets? Are all people happy when they win the lottery?*

NOTE TO PARENTS: *The lottery plays directly into a love of money. For the person who doesn't love money, the lottery has no attraction.*

Q: DOES MONEY MAKE PEOPLE BAD?

THE EVILS
OF
MONEY

HELP MY ANTI-MONEY
CAMPAIGN!
GIVE GENEROUSLY!

59

A: Money itself isn't bad, and money itself doesn't make people bad. But the *love* of money is and does. When people love money, they become greedy and do all sorts of bad things to get and keep money. God wants us to use money to help hurting people. When we hurt and use people so *we* can get money, we've got it wrong.

KEY VERSE: *For the love of money is at the root of all kinds of evil. And some people, craving money, have wandered from the faith and pierced themselves with many sorrows. (1 Timothy 6:10)*

RELATED VERSES: *Proverbs 28:25; Ezekiel 7:19; Luke 6:20, 24-25; 12:13-21; 1 John 2:15-17*

RELATED QUESTIONS: *Does money make you selfish? Money is the root of all evil, but can I do good with it? Why do fairy tales say that rich people are bad and poor people are good?*

NOTE TO PARENTS: *Try not to paint a one-sided picture of money's goodness or badness. It is true that money is a snare and a temptation to selfishness. We have to resist its negative influence; this is one reason for giving. But rich Christians have used their money to finance ministries and good works. Encourage your kids to be honest in their business dealings, pay what they owe, be generous, and use money in God's service. Using money the right way helps us keep it in perspective.*

Q: WHY CAN'T MY PARENTS JUST GET A LOAN INSTEAD OF WAITING FOR PAYDAY?

1. Parents go to the bank
2. Bank gives parents loan
3. Parents give money to Jason
4. Jason buys new bike
5. Pay Day
6. Parents pay back loan

60

A: Your parents probably could get a loan. But if they did, they would have to pay the loan back plus interest. Getting a loan doesn't really solve the problem of needing money. It just postpones the problem and makes it a little worse.

We need to learn to be patient. Usually we don't need to buy what we think we need right now. Usually we can wait a little while. It's better to wait and not borrow the money than to borrow money and buy something right now, because you'll pay more if you borrow the money.

This is why it is best to be patient. Besides, if you wait, you may get a better deal!

KEY VERSE: *And this same God who takes care of me will supply all your needs from his glorious riches, which have been given to us in Christ Jesus. (Philippians 4:19)*

RELATED VERSES: *Psalm 37:21; 118:8-9; Proverbs 3:5*

RELATED QUESTIONS: *Why can't I just buy something that I want when I like it? Why don't parents sometimes have the money to buy things?*

NOTE TO PARENTS: *Your children will remember how you handled lean times long after those times have passed. Set the pattern now. If you are strapped for money, pray as a family about it, entrust yourselves to God, and look for ways other than a quick loan to weather the storm. Do without if you can. If doing without hurts, comfort each other. Take this opportunity to point out how God has met your needs and to express confidence that he will keep on doing so, as he has promised (Philippians 4:19).*

Q: IF PEOPLE KEEP BUYING LOTS OF THINGS, WON'T THEY RUN OUT OF MONEY?

61

A: Yes. No one, not even the richest person in the world, has an unlimited supply of money. Anyone who keeps spending will run out of money sooner or later.

Some people act like they have a lot of money by borrowing a lot. They keep buying new things and buying new things and buying new things. They always seem to get whatever they want. But most of them don't really have that much money. They're just borrowing lots of it. Meanwhile, they keep having to pay more and more interest. And they pay so much for this debt that they aren't putting any money into savings. Then when they need money for college or another important expense, they don't have it.

You make a lot of *choices* about your money. Choose how much money you want to spend *before* you spend it. Make sure you set some aside for giving, saving, and paying for things you *have* to buy. Then have fun spending the rest, *and stop when it's gone.*

KEY VERSE: *Those who love pleasure become poor; wine and luxury are not the way to riches. (Proverbs 21:17)*

RELATED VERSES: *Exodus 20:17; Proverbs 13:7; James 4:1-2*

RELATED QUESTION: *Why do people live above their means?*

NOTE TO PARENTS: *This question usually arises when neighbor kids have more toys than your kids, when your kids think the neighbor kids have more, or when a neighbor spends money conspicuously. Exodus 20:17 reminds us that we must not be jealous of how others spend their money. We need to be content with what we have.*

Q: WHY DO PEOPLE SPEND MONEY THEY DON'T HAVE?

62

A: Some people do it because they can't say no to their wants. They haven't learned how to save money and wait. They have to have everything right away.

Pride is another reason. Many people think that happiness is related to how rich they are. They think that having something will make them popular. Or they believe that everyone will think they are rich if they have a new car, a new suit, or a big TV. So they buy it even if they can't afford it.

Some people spend money when they feel bad. They have no joy so they go buy something to try to make themselves feel better. But when the bills come in, they feel worse.

Try to control your spending. Overspending leads to lots of problems and makes it impossible for you to give.

KEY VERSE: *Enjoy what you have rather than desiring what you don't have. Just dreaming about nice things is meaningless; it is like chasing the wind. (Ecclesiastes 6:9)*

RELATED VERSES: *Proverbs 13:7; 25:28; Galatians 5:16-23; 2 Peter 1:6*

RELATED QUESTION: *Why do people buy things they don't need?*

NOTE TO PARENTS: *Be careful about telling a child that things don't make us happy. Things do make us happy. That is why we crave them. But things can get lost, broken, or stolen. Remind your child that nothing can take God away. No matter what happens to our things, God will always be there for us working out his plan (Romans 8:38-39).*

Q: WHAT ARE TAXES?

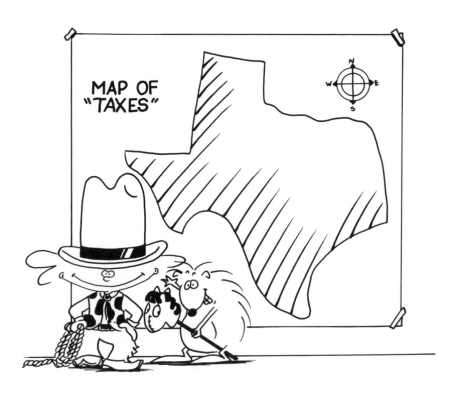

MAP OF "TAXES"

63

A: Taxes are money given to the government by the citizens of a country. It's the main way most governments get money. They use the money to run the country and provide all the services the government provides. The elected officials in the government decide how much tax people have to give. People pay income taxes (a tax on their paycheck), property taxes (a tax on the value of their house), sales taxes (a tax on items they buy), and many other kinds of taxes. The Bible tells us that we should not try to cheat the government out of taxes we owe.

KEY VERSE: *Pay your taxes, too, for these same reasons. For government workers need to be paid so they can keep on doing the work God intended them to do. (Romans 13:6)*

RELATED VERSES: *Genesis 47:23-26; Matthew 22:21; Mark 12:17; 1 Peter 2:13-14*

RELATED QUESTION: *Why do we pay taxes to the government?*

Q: WHAT DOES THE GOVERNMENT DO WITH ALL THE TAXES WE PAY?

64

A: The national government collects taxes to pay for services that they provide—highways, bridges, courtrooms, judges, military personnel, assistance for the poor, national parks, and so forth. Local governments collect taxes to pay for the services that they provide—police protection, libraries, public health, fire protection, schools, and so forth. The government uses money from taxes to provide things that all the taxpaying citizens need and want.

KEY VERSE: *A just king gives stability to his nation, but one who demands bribes destroys it. (Proverbs 29:4)*

RELATED VERSES: *Genesis 47:23-26; 1 Kings 10:11-29; Romans 13:6-7*

RELATED QUESTIONS: *Why should we pay the extra tax money to the government when they got themselves into debt? What if we don't need new roads, etc.?*

NOTE TO PARENTS: *List some of the services that taxes pay for, such as schools, libraries, streets, sewers, soldiers, sailors, police officers, and firefighters. Then pray together and thank God for these people and institutions.*

Q: WHY IS THERE SO MUCH TAX ON PRICES?

65

A: Every kind of tax pays for government services. Many local governments charge sales taxes. The amount of this tax differs from place to place. Some people think it's high because they forget that these taxes pay for a lot of the things they use every day. If you and your friends were going to buy a pizza together, it would be right for each person to pay his or her share. When you pay sales taxes, you are paying for your share of roads, schools, libraries, police officers, firefighters, and things like that. Taxes ensure that everyone in a town, city, or country pays for the things they all use.

KEY VERSES: *Each year Solomon received about twenty-five tons of gold. This did not include the additional revenue he received from merchants and traders, all the kings of Arabia, and the governors of the land. (1 Kings 10:14-15)*

RELATED VERSES: *Genesis 47:23-26; Matthew 22:17-22; Romans 13:6-7*

RELATED QUESTION: *Why is the government so unwise in its spending?*

Q: WHY SHOULD YOU PAY PROPERTY TAXES IF YOU ALREADY OWN YOUR HOUSE?

66

A: One kind of tax that local governments charge is property tax. Property taxes are paid by people who own property. Every person who owns land or buildings pays a certain amount of tax every year. The amount they pay depends on the value of their land or building. The owners of some buildings, such as churches, schools, post offices, and so forth, do not have to pay taxes. They are "tax-exempt."

The government uses property taxes to pay for things that landowners and building owners need. These include water lines, sewer service, roads, streetlights, and things like that. Even if your house is paid for, you still need these services every year. That's why you have to pay property taxes each year. It's just another way for the government to collect money from its citizens to help pay for important public services.

KEY VERSE: *[Jesus] said, "Give to Caesar what belongs to him. But everything that belongs to God must be given to God." (Matthew 22:21)*

RELATED VERSES: *Genesis 47:23-26; Matthew 17:27; 22:17-22; Romans 13:6-7*

RELATED QUESTION: *Why can't the government pay its own bills?*

NOTE TO PARENTS: *It is easy for people to forget that they are part of a community that depends on the cooperation of all its members. The services provided by property taxes benefit everyone.*

Q: WHY DO PEOPLE GET BORED WITH SOMETHING THEY JUST BOUGHT?

67

A: People get bored quickly with something new that they just bought because they thought it would be better than it is. They may have believed the commercials that said the product would be exciting, but it really wasn't. When they finally got the product, it wasn't what they thought it would be. For example, they may have seen a game that looked like fun for the whole family to play. But what looked good on TV really wasn't very good at all.

Some people expect a product to do more than it can. A girl might think that a special dress will make her popular. Or a boy might think that a certain brand of basketball shoes will make him a better player. Then they discover the truth.

Many people "impulse buy." They go into a store not planning to buy anything, but then they see something they want and change their mind. They didn't plan to buy it, but it looked good in the store. Then later they wonder why they ever bought this thing that they don't need.

KEY VERSE: *Then [Jesus] said, "Beware! Don't be greedy for what you don't have. Real life is not measured by how much we own." (Luke 12:15)*

RELATED VERSES: *Matthew 6:24; Philippians 4:12; Hebrews 11:25; 13:5; 1 John 2:16*

RELATED QUESTION: *Why are people never happy with what they have?*

Q: WHY DO PEOPLE WASTE THEIR MONEY ON DUMB THINGS?

68

A: Some purchases really are dumb, but people make them because at the time they think they need whatever they buy. They may waste their money because they believe the advertisements. Maybe they want to have what their friends have. Or maybe they just don't value their money and don't mind throwing it away.

But be careful about calling someone's decision dumb. Sometimes what may seem dumb to you is really smart. Remember, you don't know the other person's situation in life or his or her needs. So don't judge others for what they buy. They may think that you waste your money on some of the things you buy. It's easy to criticize someone else's spending.

KEY VERSE: *Stop judging others, and you will not be judged. Stop criticizing others, or it will all come back on you. If you forgive others, you will be forgiven. (Luke 6:37)*

RELATED VERSES: *Luke 6:41-42; James 5:19-20*

RELATED QUESTION: *Why do people spend so much money on things if they will just lose it all when they die?*

NOTE TO PARENTS: *Try not to criticize how others spend their money. It is an unhealthy habit that cultivates the wrong type of attitudes about other people. And if you do it, so will your kids.*

GIVE ME SOME CREDIT

Q: ARE CREDIT CARDS GOOD OR BAD?

OBEDIENCE
SCHOOL
Credit Cards
Welcome

CREDIT
CARD
$$1.98

69

A: They're both. Credit cards are good because they provide a very easy way to buy things. People can buy things they want without having to carry cash or a checkbook. People can also buy things over the phone and through the mail using credit cards. Some credit cards can be used in bank machines and can be used for borrowing money from a bank.

But credit cards can be bad because they make it easy for people to buy things that they can't afford or should not buy. In fact, many people use credit cards to spend *much* more than they should. When you spend too much and can't pay the whole bill, the credit-card company lets you make a small payment and charges you a lot of interest on what you don't pay. Misusing credit cards has put many people deeply in debt.

The right way to use a credit card is to use it only for things you have planned and budgeted to buy. Then you know you can pay the whole amount when the bill comes.

KEY VERSE: *Just as the rich rule the poor, so the borrower is servant to the lender. (Proverbs 22:7)*

RELATED VERSES: *Psalm 37:21; Matthew 6:19-21, 24-34*

RELATED QUESTION: *Why do some people not like credit cards?*

NOTE TO PARENTS: *If you have a credit-card bill with a finance charge on it, show it to your child. Explain that this charge is the extra money you have to pay for using a credit card and not paying the bill in full right away.*

Q: HOW DO CREDIT CARDS WORK?

70

A: A credit card lets you borrow money from a bank whenever you want to buy something. The bank gives you the card and says you can borrow a certain amount of money. When you want to buy something with the credit card, the salesclerk checks to make sure that you have permission to borrow that much money. The clerk also makes sure you are using your *own* card and not someone else's. If everything checks out OK, the *bank*, not you, pays for the item. The bank loans you the money. The salesclerk lets you take home what you wanted to buy.

A little while later, a bill for the amount you borrowed comes in the mail. You have to pay this bill right away. If you don't, the bank charges you extra money called interest. This is how most people get in trouble with credit cards. They borrow more than they can pay back. Then the interest payments get higher and higher. Sometimes people borrow so much that they can't possibly pay it back. Wise people borrow only as much as they know they can pay back.

KEY VERSES: *Do not co-sign another person's note or put up a guarantee for someone else's loan. If you can't pay it, even your bed will be snatched from under you. (Proverbs 22:26-27)*

RELATED VERSES: *Luke 16:10-13*

RELATED QUESTIONS: *When you use a credit card, why do you have to pay the money afterwards? What are credit cards for?*

NOTE TO PARENTS: *To many kids, credit cards give the appearance that you can get something without paying. It's important to explain that you do have to pay.*

Q: WHY CAN'T I HAVE MY OWN CREDIT CARD?

71

A: It is against the law for children to have their own credit cards. That's because children don't have regular jobs, and most children don't have much money. How would they pay the bills without any money?

Children can have debit cards, though. Debit cards are just as easy to use as credit cards. You can buy anything, anywhere, anytime. But the money comes right out of your bank account instead of a loan from the bank. You never borrow any money because you spend only what is in your account. You still need to be responsible and spend only the amount you planned to spend. If you are responsible with your budget and your saving and spending, perhaps your parents will let you have a debit card.

KEY VERSE: *"Well done!" the king exclaimed. "You are a trustworthy servant. You have been faithful with the little I entrusted to you, so you will be governor of ten cities as your reward." (Luke 19:17)*

RELATED VERSES: *Matthew 25:14-30; Luke 12:15; 1 John 2:15*

RELATED QUESTIONS: *Why do you have to be a certain age to get a credit card? Why don't my parents let me have a credit card?*

NOTE TO PARENTS: *Emphasize the tie between responsibility and privilege. The person who can spend a little money wisely will be given more money to manage later. You can encourage your child to handle money wisely by affirming and rewarding wise use of his or her allowance.*

Q: WHAT HAPPENS IF A PERSON DOESN'T PAY A CREDIT-CARD BILL?

72

A: A person who doesn't pay a credit-card bill on time is charged interest. Sometimes the bank will charge extra penalty fees too. If someone goes for a long time without paying off a credit-card bill, the small bill will turn into a huge one.

People who don't pay *anything* on their credit-card bills get in big trouble with their bank. Not paying credit-card bills goes on a person's credit record. It shows that the person cannot be trusted with money. That will hurt the person if he or she ever wants to get a loan from a bank.

It also displeases God. God wants us to always be honest and do what we say we are going to do. When we don't pay the bills we agreed to pay, we are being dishonest. It is important that we borrow money only if we know we can pay it back.

KEY VERSE: *The wicked borrow and never repay, but the godly are generous givers. (Psalm 37:21)*

RELATED VERSES: *Leviticus 19:13; Proverbs 22:3; Luke 16:10-13*

RELATED QUESTIONS: *Why do you have to pay someone back if you borrow money? Why is there a national debt—why don't they just call it off?*

NOTE TO PARENTS: *Explain the difference between credit and debt. Credit is when someone is willing to lend you a certain amount of money. Credit is good to have. It shows that others trust you. When we use credit for convenience and within our budget, it is a good thing. Debt is when you owe money to someone else. Debt is not wrong, but it can cause problems and therefore should be avoided as much as possible.*

Q: IS IT WRONG TO BORROW MONEY?

73

A: It is not a *sin* to borrow money; it's just not very smart. God gave rules to the Israelites for loaning money to each other, so obviously it was OK for them to do it. You can find those rules in the Bible (Deuteronomy 15:1-11; 23:19-20; 24:10-13).

Although it isn't wrong, borrowing money is not the best thing to do. Borrowing money from a bank will cost you interest charges. Borrowing money from a friend may cost you a friendship. That's because you may forget or be unable to pay back your friend, and he or she may get mad.

Sometimes borrowing money is necessary, such as when someone wants to buy a house. But a lot of people borrow in order to buy things they really don't need. If you really want something, try to save up for it first. If you can't save up for it, maybe you need to get along without it.

KEY VERSE: *A prudent person foresees the danger ahead and takes precautions; the simpleton goes blindly on and suffers the consequences. (Proverbs 22:3)*

RELATED VERSES: *Psalm 37:21; Proverbs 22:7; Matthew 6:19-21, 24-34*

NOTE TO PARENTS: *Be willing to give your children credit: If you are out together and they want to buy something but have not brought their spending money, buy it for them and have them pay you back when you get home. But avoid lending them money against future income, since borrowing is a foolish habit to develop. (Save the word wrong for issues such as lying and cheating. Borrowing is not wrong; it's just not the ideal way to buy things.)*

Q: WHY DO PEOPLE HAVE TO PAY INTEREST ON MONEY THEY BORROW?

74

A: People have to pay interest only if they agree to do so when they borrow the money. All credit cards come with a contract that tells exactly how much the user of the card has to pay. When people borrow money from a bank, they sign an agreement that explains how much interest they will pay. Banks charge interest on loans and credit cards because that's how they make money. Paying interest to a bank is like paying rent. You want to use the money for a while, so you pay the bank for that privilege.

When God gave the Law to the Israelites, he told them not to charge each other interest for loans. Today many people will loan money to relatives and close friends without charging interest to help them in an emergency.

KEY VERSES: *If any of your Israelite relatives fall into poverty and cannot support themselves, support them as you would a resident foreigner and allow them to live with you. Do not demand an advance or charge interest on the money you lend them. Instead, show your fear of God by letting them live with you as your relatives. Remember, do not charge your relatives interest on anything you lend them, whether money or food. (Leviticus 25:35-37)*

RELATED VERSES: *Exodus 22:25; Deuteronomy 15:6; 23:19-20; Ezekiel 18:8*

RELATED QUESTIONS: *Do you have to pay more money each time you don't pay your credit-card bill? How come banks charge interest when you borrow money from them?*

Q: WHAT IS A MORTGAGE?

75

A: A mortgage is an agreement to pay back a loan that is secured with a piece of property. The agreement says that the borrower will pay back the loan over a certain period of time and at a certain rate of interest. It also says that the bank can take possession of the property and sell it if the borrower does not pay back the loan as agreed.

This is how most people buy a house. Houses cost a lot of money. Most people do not have enough money to pay for a house all at once, so they borrow the money from a bank. The agreement between the home buyer and the bank is the mortgage.

Most people repay their home loans by paying a little each month. Then after fifteen to thirty years, the whole loan is paid back, the mortgage is canceled, and the house is paid for.

KEY VERSE: *But the man fell down before the king and begged him, "Oh, sir, be patient with me, and I will pay it all." (Matthew 18:26)*

RELATED VERSE: *Genesis 47:20*

RELATED QUESTION: *What if you need to buy a house and you don't have the money?*

Q: WHY ARE THERE BILLS TO PAY?

76

A: A bill is simply a charge for something you bought or used but haven't paid for yet. Most people get bills for water, electricity, telephone service, gas, magazines, and things like that. Because your family used gas for the water heater, electricity for the lights, and water to drink, you have to pay for them.

KEY VERSE: *Do not cheat or rob anyone. Always pay your hired workers promptly. (Leviticus 19:13)*

RELATED QUESTIONS: *Does God want us to have bills? Why do people pay bills?*

NOTE TO PARENTS: *This question often arises when bills become the focus of attention, such as when they come in the mail or when a parent blames them for making money tight. Simply explain what bills are and how the family benefits from the things they buy—the water you drink, the electricity that keeps the refrigerator going and the lights on, the house and furnace that keep you warm, and the book bag you bought last week to carry your books. In other words, help your children appreciate the value of paying the bills rather than seeing them only as impediments to getting what they want.*

Q: WHAT IF I DON'T HAVE ENOUGH MONEY TO PAY MY BILLS?

77

A: It is very important to pay your bills. Paying what you owe is part of being honest and trustworthy. If for some reason you lose your money or run out of money, you need to work out a plan for paying what you owe. Your plan should involve getting more money and spending less. You may have to sell some of what you own. You will also need to talk to the people whom you owe and see if they will let you pay little by little. See if you can work out a way to pay them each a small amount every week or month until the bills are all paid off.

This is not a good situation to be in. If you learn to budget, save, tithe, and spend wisely, you may never have to go through it. That is why it is important to follow God's guidelines. God knows how things work best, and his way is always best.

KEY VERSES: *When the people of Egypt and Canaan ran out of money, they came to Joseph crying again for food. . . . The next year they came again and said, "Our money is gone, and our livestock are yours. We have nothing left but our bodies and land. Why should we die before your very eyes? Buy us and our land in exchange for food; we will then become servants to Pharaoh." (Genesis 47:15, 18-19)*

RELATED VERSES: *Leviticus 19:13; 2 Kings 4:7; Proverbs 14:23; 21:20; 22:3; 24:3; 27:23-24*

RELATED QUESTION: *Why do you have to pay bills?*

Q: SHOULD I BORROW MONEY FROM THE BANK OR FROM MY FRIENDS?

78

A: It's better not to borrow at all. Save your own money until you have enough for what you need. Or pray for a way to earn extra money and look for work you can do. If you must borrow for some emergency, make sure you sign a written agreement, even if the money comes from a friend. Then pay it back as soon as you can.

But try not to borrow from friends. It could easily lead to arguments, and Proverbs makes it clear that arguments can separate close friends. It's better not to put your friends under this kind of pressure.

If a friend wants to borrow from you, it is best just to give it as a gift. Or if you do make a loan, think of it as a gift. That way you will never worry about whether it gets paid back. If someone does not pay you back, forgive the person right away and forget it.

KEY VERSE: *Do not charge interest on the loans you make to a fellow Israelite, whether it is money, food, or anything else that may be loaned with interest. (Deuteronomy 23:19)*

RELATED VERSES: *Exodus 22:10-15; Deuteronomy 24:13-17; Proverbs 6:1-5; 18:19*

RELATED QUESTION: *Is it true that money can break up friends?*

NOTE TO PARENTS: *Tell your kids not to borrow money from friends. Good friends are hard to find and even harder to replace; losing them over a money-related squabble is not worth it.*

FROM
ALLOWANCE
TO
PAYCHECK

Q: WHY DO SOME KIDS GET THEIR ALLOWANCE FREE AND OTHERS HAVE TO EARN IT?

79

A: Every family is different. In some families, children have to do jobs around the house to earn their allowances. In other families, children receive money just for being part of the family. Some don't get any allowance at all. It's all up to the parents.

Be careful about comparing your parents and family with others. God has given your mother and father the responsibility of rearing you, not your friends. And your friends' parents are not in charge of you.

What really matters is how you deal with your own situation. God wants you to learn to manage your money wisely. He also wants you to be a good worker and learn how to be a valuable member of a team. Whether the two are tied together doesn't matter as much as what you need to learn from them.

KEY VERSE: *Work brings profit, but mere talk leads to poverty! (Proverbs 14:23)*

RELATED VERSE: *Ecclesiastes 7:11*

RELATED QUESTIONS: *Why do moms and dads give you less money for a job than someone else? How come some parents give their children allowances if their children don't even do anything? Why do we get allowances if we don't do any work?*

NOTE TO PARENTS: *Try not to tie allowances to chores. Doing so gives children the impression that they should be paid for all work, even cleaning up after themselves. Give them both chores and an allowance because they are part of the family.*

Q: WHY DO SOME KIDS GET HUGE ALLOWANCES AND OTHERS DON'T GET ANY?

80

A: Allowances vary a lot among kids for many different reasons. Some families have lots of money, and others have very little. Some parents have no money left after paying the bills, so their children get no allowance—the money just isn't there.

Remember also that some parents give their children money in other ways besides allowances. They may give money for doing special work around the house. Or some parents may give their kids a large amount of money and let them buy all their own clothes.

Every family is different—different personalities and different situations. In fact, no other family is exactly like yours. Thank God for your family and make the most of it. God will always supply what you need.

KEY VERSE: *Fix your thoughts on what is true and honorable and right. Think about things that are pure and lovely and admirable. Think about things that are excellent and worthy of praise. (Philippians 4:8)*

RELATED VERSES: *Genesis 4:6-7; Proverbs 14:23; Matthew 20:15; Luke 15:12-14; Philippians 4:11-13, 18-19; Hebrews 13:5*

RELATED QUESTIONS: *Why don't I get an allowance? Shouldn't I get an allowance?*

NOTE TO PARENTS: *It is important that your children get money of their own through one means or another so they can begin to learn how to handle money wisely.*

Q: HOW COME I DON'T GET ENOUGH ALLOWANCE TO BUY ANYTHING?

81

A: You can always buy *something* with the money you have, even if it's very little. You may think you don't have enough money to buy anything when you look at your allowance, but just because you can't buy *expensive* things doesn't mean you can't buy *anything*.

Some people want to buy just about everything they see, so they never have enough money. Don't be like that. Instead, learn to be content with what you have. If there is something you want and your parents agree that you can have it, save your money until you have enough to buy it. Be patient. You can also ask God for opportunities to earn extra money.

———————————————————————————

KEY VERSE: *I know how to live on almost nothing or with everything. I have learned the secret of living in every situation, whether it is with a full stomach or empty, with plenty or little. (Philippians 4:12)*

RELATED VERSES: *Proverbs 14:23; 22:29; Ecclesiastes 7:8; Luke 12:15; Galatians 5:22; 1 Thessalonians 5:14; Hebrews 13:5; 1 John 2:15-17*

RELATED QUESTIONS: *Why do I only get $3 a week? I cut the lawn, rake it, clean my room, and other stuff, so I should get more, shouldn't I? Why is an allowance so little, like $2?*

NOTE TO PARENTS: *When your kids feel that they can't buy the things they really want, teach them to ask God for the things they want and to save diligently. It's best not to increase allowances or buy them what they want all the time.*

Q: WHY DO KIDS GET LESS MONEY THAN ADULTS?

82

A: The more you can do, the more you can earn. Adults earn more than kids because they can do more. They get paid for the *skills* they have learned. The older they get, the better they are at doing their work, and the more they get paid for it. And the more skill their job takes, the more they get paid.

For example, repairing a car, being a doctor, keeping financial records, closing a sale, and writing a book are all difficult jobs. They take a lot of skill. Only people who have been trained and have the experience can do them well. And those people are paid well for the work they do.

Also, many adult jobs carry great responsibility. A person who runs a store has to take care of all the workers, all the products in the store, and the building. That's a lot of responsibility. People are paid according to how much *responsibility* they have.

Be glad you don't have to earn as much as an adult. Adults make more money than kids, but they also have many more bills and many more responsibilities.

As time goes on, you will learn how to do many jobs through skills, training, and experience. Eventually you will get to serve God in a job that uses your abilities. Your responsibilities and your income will increase bit by bit as you continue to get more training and experience. *Then* you will be able to think about getting more money and things.

KEY VERSE: *Do you see any truly competent workers? They will serve kings rather than ordinary people. (Proverbs 22:29)*

RELATED VERSES: *Proverbs 14:23; Matthew 25:21; Luke 19:17*

RELATED QUESTION: *Why don't kids have as much money as adults?*

Q: HOW ARE KIDS SUPPOSED TO EARN MONEY?

83

A: Kids can earn money by doing work for their parents and neighbors. Maybe you can clean up the yard, wash dishes, wash the car, or run errands. Most adults like to pay kids for doing those kinds of jobs.

You can also start your own business. Make something that you can sell, or provide a service such as gardening, lawn care, or delivery. Ask your parents and God for ideas and for good opportunities.

If you really want to earn money, do every job well and always do more than is expected of you. Think about what you're doing, keep going until you're done, and never complain.

KEY VERSES: *Work hard and cheerfully at whatever you do, as though you were working for the Lord rather than for people. Remember that the Lord will give you an inheritance as your reward, and the Master you are serving is Christ. (Colossians 3:23-24)*

RELATED VERSES: *Psalm 90:17; Proverbs 14:23; Philippians 2:14*

RELATED QUESTIONS: *What job can I get now that I am ten? How old do you have to be to work for money?*

NOTE TO PARENTS: *Giving children small jobs to do is a good way to introduce them to work. Make a job list and post jobs that need to be done and how much you are willing to pay for each. Let your children know they can pick jobs off the list once their regular chores are done. Give clear instructions, show the child what to do, and make sure he or she understands what you expect to find when it is done. Don't forget to give praise for a job well done.*

Q: WHERE DOES THE MONEY THAT BOSSES PAY COME FROM?

84

A: Every company sells something. Bosses get money from the people who buy a company's products or services. The money that comes from these sales pays the workers—all of them, from the bosses to the people who work for the bosses. It works like this: If you owned a field of pumpkins, you could sell the pumpkins for $10 each. So if you had 100 pumpkins, you would have $1,000 if you sold them all. Out of that money, you would pay your workers—the people who helped pick and sell the pumpkins. You would have to plan well in order to have enough money to be fair to your workers, to pay your other expenses, and to make a profit. That's how companies work.

KEY VERSE: *At that time, Egyptian chariots delivered to Jerusalem could be purchased for 600 pieces of silver, and horses could be bought for 150 pieces of silver. Many of these were then resold to the kings of the Hittites and the kings of Aram. (1 Kings 10:29)*

RELATED VERSES: *Leviticus 19:13; Psalm 128:2; Proverbs 14:23; Matthew 20:1-16*

RELATED QUESTION: *Where does all the money go?*

NOTE TO PARENTS: *You can help your children start a small business of their own. Help them plan their costs, sale price, and profits. Whether your children ever go into business for themselves or not, this will help them learn how a business works.*

Q: WHAT DOES MINIMUM WAGE MEAN?

85

A: The minimum wage is the smallest amount that a business is allowed to pay a person for one hour of work. The government decides that amount. It's a law.

When God gave the Law to the Israelites, he told them to pay their workers fairly. That's what it means when it says, "Do not keep an ox from eating as it treads out the grain" (Deuteronomy 25:4). A good boss pays his or her workers fairly.

KEY VERSE: *For the Scripture says, "Do not keep an ox from eating as it treads out the grain." And in another place, "Those who work deserve their pay!" (1 Timothy 5:18)*

RELATED VERSES: *Leviticus 19:13; Deuteronomy 15:18; 24:14-15; Nehemiah 5:1-7; Proverbs 12:24; Matthew 20:1-16; 1 Corinthians 9:9-10*

RELATED QUESTION: *Why are kids paid minimum wage?*

NOTE TO PARENTS: *When you are paying your children to do jobs, make sure you pay them fairly, in keeping with the jobs and their skill levels. Paying them too much can give them unrealistic expectations that they will carry with them into the workforce. Paying them too little can discourage them.*

Q: SHOULD PEOPLE STAY AT A GOOD-PAYING JOB THAT THEY DON'T LIKE?

86

A: Whether or not a person should stay in a yucky job depends on the person and the job. What matters most is doing what God wants. When you become an adult and have a family, God will want you to take care of them. You will need to work so you can pay for food, clothes, housing, and other bills. You may have to stay in a job you don't like so you can do this.

That doesn't mean that you *must* have a job you don't like. God loves you and has a plan for your life. If you follow his guidance and do what he says, he will lead you to a good job and make you content. He doesn't want you to be miserable.

No one has a job that he or she enjoys in *every way, all the time*. Every job is hard—and maybe even yucky!—sometimes. That is why it is important to learn to be content.

Pray now about your future job. Give your life to God's service. Ask God to guide you in your education. Trust God to help you find work that suits how he made you. Life on earth will never be perfect, and you may not always have a fun job. But if you do what God wants you to do, do your duty to your family, and be content with what you have, God will take care of you.

KEY VERSE: *"For I know the plans I have for you," says the Lord. "They are plans for good and not for disaster, to give you a future and a hope." (Jeremiah 29:11)*

RELATED VERSES: *Deuteronomy 30:9-10; Proverbs 6:6-11; 14:23; Ecclesiastes 7:14*

RELATED QUESTION: *If you take a job that pays lots of money, are you being greedy?*

Q: WHAT SHOULD PEOPLE DO IF THEY DO NOT GET PAID ENOUGH AT THEIR JOB?

GARAGE
SALE
THIS
SATURDAY

87

A: The first thing these people should do is ask God to provide for them. Then they can ask the boss for overtime, do some extra part-time work, or look for another job that pays better.

But it's important to realize that many people *think* they do not get paid enough when they really do. Every month, their bills seem to grow, and they don't know how they can pay everyone. The real problem is that they spend too much. Even people who make a *lot* of money can have this problem. They need to budget their money and control their spending better.

Some people don't make very much but still manage to pay all their bills. They have learned to budget their money and control their spending so they never spend more than they earn.

No matter how much you get paid, a lot depends on what you do with your money. You can often have enough if you budget your money and spend less than you earn.

KEY VERSE: *Work brings profit, but mere talk leads to poverty! (Proverbs 14:23)*

RELATED VERSES: *Proverbs 6:6-11; Amos 4:1-3; Ephesians 6:7-8; Philippians 4:19; Colossians 3:23-24; 1 Timothy 5:8*

RELATED QUESTION: *If you got a job and you knew they weren't paying you enough, what should you do?*

NOTE TO PARENTS: *Live within your means and help your children do the same. It's the same principle with $5 as it is with $5,000.*

Q: WHY DO ATHLETES GET PAID SO MUCH MONEY TO DO SOMETHING THAT'S FUN?

1. CONTRACTS
2. T.V. RIGHTS
3. ENDORSEMENTS
4. COMMERCIALS

COACH

88

A: In this country, people enjoy professional sports so much that basketball, football, baseball, hockey, golf, and other sports have become big businesses. Millions of people pay a lot of money for tickets to the games. Television networks pay millions of dollars for the right to show games. Sports fans spend countless dollars on shirts, caps, and other things. So sports stars ask for big salaries, and they usually get them.

But it's not all fun. To be excellent in a sport takes years of hard work and training. Many professional athletes suffer many cuts, bruises, and broken bones.

It doesn't seem right that athletes get paid so much for playing a game, especially when teachers and ministers do more important work and get paid much less. But life isn't always fair. Often the world has things backwards.

KEY VERSE: *I have observed something else in this world of ours. The fastest runner doesn't always win the race, and the strongest warrior doesn't always win the battle. The wise are often poor, and the skillful are not necessarily wealthy. And those who are educated don't always lead successful lives. It is all decided by chance, by being at the right place at the right time. (Ecclesiastes 9:11)*

RELATED VERSES: *Exodus 20:17; Proverbs 22:29; Ecclesiastes 8:14; Luke 12:15*

RELATED QUESTION: *Is it fair that some people work hard and barely make it while others do almost nothing and live like kings?*

NOTE TO PARENTS: *Point out to your child that athletes got where they are by working hard. They practiced day after day for years before they became professionals, and they keep on practicing. They practice whether or not they feel like it.*

Q: HOW WILL I KNOW WHAT I WANT TO DO WHEN I GROW UP?

89

A: It is good to think about what you want to do when you grow up. God has made you good at doing certain things. He has given you talents, interests, and abilities. As you get older, you will learn more and more about your abilities. Your parents and other people who know you well will help you uncover and develop your talents.

But don't wait for them to tell you what to do. Whenever you get interested in something or do well in something, keep working at it. Find out more about it. Ask questions about it. Read books about it. Take an extra class. Ask God to guide you and keep learning.

God has a plan for your life. He created you and loves you. He knows exactly what you will be best at and enjoy most and where you fit in his plan. Keep asking God to direct you, and he will do it.

KEY VERSE: *If you need wisdom—if you want to know what God wants you to do—ask him, and he will gladly tell you. He will not resent your asking. (James 1:5)*

RELATED VERSES: *Psalm 139:16; Proverbs 3:5-6; Jeremiah 29:11; Ephesians 2:10*

RELATED QUESTION: *How will you know what job is right for you?*

NOTE TO PARENTS: *Avoid telling kids that they should pursue a certain career for the money or because of some ambition of your own. Children need to seek God and pursue his plan for their lives even if it does not follow in a parent's footsteps or make up for a parent's lost opportunity.*

WHEN THE BUDGET WON'T BUDGE

Q: WHAT IS BUDGETING?

90

A: A budget is a plan for how to use your money. If you knew you would be receiving $10, for example, you might decide ahead of time to put aside $1 for church and $2 in your savings account in the bank. You might also decide to put $4 in your jar to use in two weeks for a church camping trip. The final $3 you might decide to carry with you to spend on snacks. That plan would be your budget.

It's a good idea to write down your budget so you always know how to divide your money. Start with at least three categories: tithe, savings, and spending money. Then you can add others as your needs change. You could include one, like in the example above, for an upcoming church camping trip.

A budget is also a good way of tracking your spending. After you have spent the money, you can compare what you did to how you planned to spend it. That helps you plan better in the future.

KEY VERSE: *A prudent person foresees the danger ahead and takes precautions; the simpleton goes blindly on and suffers the consequences. (Proverbs 22:3)*

RELATED VERSES: *Proverbs 21:20; 22:3; 24:3*

RELATED QUESTION: *Why do people have so much money when they have to buy only a few things?*

NOTE TO PARENTS: *The best time for children to practice managing money is when they are young. And one of the best ways to give them practice is to give them an allowance. Help your child set up a budget that makes sense for him or her.*

Q: WHY DO PEOPLE HAVE TO BUDGET THEIR MONEY?

91

A: People should budget their money so they will have enough for all the bills they must pay. Everyone has big bills that come due in the future. It is good to write them down as a reminder so you won't be surprised when they come. The budget tells you how much to set aside each week or month so that you will have the money to pay the bills when they come.

Every day brings opportunities to spend money—opportunities to buy something that you didn't plan for. A budget helps you know whether or not you can afford it.

You don't *have* to budget your money. You can just go and spend it. But if you do, you will probably run out of money too soon. Then you will not have enough for the things you need, and you will never get to spend your money on the things you really want. Everyone should have a plan for how to spend his or her money.

KEY VERSE: *The wise have wealth and luxury, but fools spend whatever they get. (Proverbs 21:20)*

RELATED VERSES: *Proverbs 22:3; 23:19-21*

RELATED QUESTIONS: *Why don't they just make everything cheaper, and people would be rich and happy? Why don't they just make dollars worth more?*

NOTE TO PARENTS: *To illustrate the need for budgeting, sit down one evening with your child and list all the things he or she would like to have. Then write down what each item would cost, total them, and compare this with how much he or she has to spend over the next month. The only way to keep from running out of money is to look at this list and plan!*

Q: WHY CAN'T PARENTS AFFORD A LOT OF THINGS?

1. Tithe
2. TOYS
3. GAMES
4. POP & CANDY
5. Other: food
    rent
    bills

92

A: Parents can't afford to spend money on certain things because they have chosen to spend their money on other things. All people have bills to pay with a limited amount of money. And all people have to make choices about how they will spend that money. When your parents say they can't afford to buy something you want, it's probably because it is not in their budget, not because they don't have any money.

That may sound unfair, but it's really wise planning. People should say no to some things so they can have enough for the things they need and want most.

If the thing you need is really important, ask your parents nicely if they will include it in their budget as soon as they can. If it's something you just want badly, put it into *your* budget. Then you can start earning money and saving for it.

KEY VERSE: *Those who love pleasure become poor; wine and luxury are not the way to riches. (Proverbs 21:17)*

RELATED VERSES: *Galatians 5:22-23; Philippians 4:12*

RELATED QUESTION: *I want a volleyball net and I know my parents have the money, but they just say it's too much money. What should I do?*

NOTE TO PARENTS: *If your child is old enough, show him or her your budget. Explain that this is what you must spend money on and that this is why you sometimes say, "We can't afford that"—it's another way of saying, "We need the money for other things" (food, clothes, an upcoming vacation or birthday party, a home repair, savings for college, and so on).*

Q: WHY DO SOME PEOPLE SPEND EVERY CENT THEY GET RIGHT AWAY?

93

A: Some people spend all their money right away because they have no self-control. They have no discipline or patience. They can't wait even though they should. They don't save money because they convince themselves that they have to buy things they don't really need.

This is not good. God wants his people to be self-controlled so they will use well what he has given them. God also wants people to take care of each other. It would be wrong for parents to spend all their money on themselves and forget about the children or the house payment. It would be wrong for Christians to spend all their money on themselves and neglect the church. It would be wrong for the boss to spend all the company's money on himself and not pay the workers.

We need to control our spending, not let our spending control us.

KEY VERSE: *The wise have wealth and luxury, but fools spend whatever they get. (Proverbs 21:20)*

RELATED VERSES: *Matthew 6:19-21; Luke 3:14; 12:20; Philippians 4:11-13; 1 Timothy 6:8; Hebrews 13:5; 1 John 2:16*

RELATED QUESTION: *Do more than 50 percent of people spend their money wisely?*

NOTE TO PARENTS: *If your children overspend, do not bail them out by giving or lending them more money. Let them learn the truth: overspending hurts.*

Q: WHY DO PEOPLE SPEND THEIR MONEY ON LITTLE THINGS AND NOT ON THE IMPORTANT THINGS?

94

A:

Some people waste their money because they are foolish. They don't care about what really matters, so they spend money on worthless things. They don't love God or don't know what is important to him. Some don't think about the future enough.

Some people simply never make a plan for how to spend their money. They just spend until the money is gone. They may want important things, but they can't get them because they have no plan.

Others only *seem* to spend money on things that are not important. These people are just different from you, not foolish. What is unimportant to you is important to them.

Be careful not to judge others who spend differently. Not every small item is unimportant. It may be that what others buy is important after all—just not important to you.

KEY VERSE: *So be careful not to jump to conclusions before the Lord returns as to whether or not someone is faithful. When the Lord comes, he will bring our deepest secrets to light and will reveal our private motives. And then God will give to everyone whatever praise is due. (1 Corinthians 4:5)*

RELATED VERSES: *Matthew 7:1; Luke 6:37; Galatians 5:16-17*

RELATED QUESTION: *Why do the weirdest things cost so much money?*

NOTE TO PARENTS: *Be careful about judging how your neighbor spends his or her money. But you can explain to your child that some purchases are more foolish than others.*

Q: WHY IS IT THAT WHEN I WANT TO BUY SOMETHING I AM ALWAYS SHORT OF CASH?

95

A: If you want to buy something but don't have enough money, you probably decided to buy it at the last minute, before you had time to save money for it. It's OK to buy small things that way as long as you have enough spending money. But if it costs more, you need to plan and save to buy it. So you aren't really short of cash; you just can't buy everything right away. That's why we need to learn to save.

Sometimes you save up for something, but it costs more than you thought it would. Check on the price of what you want to buy before you go to the store. That way you will know whether you have enough money. Remember also that you have to pay tax on just about everything. You have to add tax to the price before you can buy it.

KEY VERSE: *Wise people think before they act; fools don't and even brag about it! (Proverbs 13:16)*

RELATED VERSE: *Luke 14:28*

RELATED QUESTIONS: *Why do things cost so much money? What if you buy lots of things and run out of money?*

NOTE TO PARENTS: *If your child really wants something but doesn't have enough spending money, resist the temptation to make up the difference or loan the money. Help your child wait until he or she has saved the money. Children need to learn to plan their purchases and stay on budget.*

Q: DOES GOD GET ANGRY WHEN I SPEND MY MONEY FOOLISHLY?

96

A: Does he rant and rave? No. But God does want us to be wise, and he's sad when we are foolish. Think of it this way: God is your biggest fan. More than anyone else, he wants you to win. That's why he cares about how you take care of your money. If you keep wasting it and ignoring wise advice from everybody all the time, *of course* he will be sad, because things won't go as well for you.

KEY VERSE: *And do not bring sorrow to God's Holy Spirit by the way you live. Remember, he is the one who has identified you as his own, guaranteeing that you will be saved on the day of redemption. (Ephesians 4:30)*

RELATED VERSES: *Jeremiah 13:17; Joel 2:13*

RELATED QUESTION: *When you buy something that you don't have enough for but it is for a Christian use, will God bless you for it and provide?*

NOTE TO PARENTS: *Don't use fear of angering God as a tool for getting your child to behave. Emphasize God's care for your child, not his punishment. Meanwhile, demonstrate what you mean by controlling your own anger when your child makes a foolish money decision. Give your child room for making mistakes without blowing your top.*

Q:

HOW DO I KNOW WHAT IS WISE TO SPEND MY MONEY ON?

97

A: The Bible explains that it is important to give to the church and to help people in need, to pay bills that you promised to pay, and to buy things that you need. It is always wise to spend money that way.

It is also wise to use your money for the most important things first and the least important things last. Here they are in order: (1) Giving to the church. (2) Paying for commitments you made. (3) Taking care of your needs. (4) Saving. (5) Spending for things you would like. If you want to spend money on something you would like, make sure you have done the other four things first.

It is also wise to get a good deal. Never buy something just because it looks good, just because you saw it advertised on TV, or just because your friends have it. Buy things that are good quality and have a reasonable price.

Whenever you want to buy something, ask, *Do I really need it?* If you're unsure, ask God for wisdom, and wait awhile before deciding. Ask your parents because God gives them wisdom too.

KEY VERSE: *If you need wisdom—if you want to know what God wants you to do—ask him, and he will gladly tell you. He will not resent your asking. (James 1:5)*

RELATED VERSES: *1 Kings 12:6-8; Proverbs 1:8-9; 12:26; 13:20; 24:3-6; Galatians 5:16; James 3:17-18*

NOTE TO PARENTS: *You may need to explain the difference between necessities and luxuries. You may also want to go over a list of priorities you use for evaluating purchases: Is it something I need? Will it last? Have I shopped for the best price? Should I save the money instead and get something of better value later?*

HONESTY
IS THE
BEST POLICY

Q: WOULD IT BE RIGHT TO KEEP THE MONEY IF SOMEONE PAID TOO MUCH?

98

A: No. Suppose you sold something to a friend, and the friend paid you too much by mistake. You should give back the extra money. That's just being honest and fair. And isn't that the way you would want to be treated? You should be truthful and honest with people—just the way you want them to be truthful and honest with you.

Also, you shouldn't cheat people by charging them too much for something. God told his people not to take advantage of each other, and he had harsh words for people who broke this rule. Some people say, "If the person doesn't notice, then it's his own fault." But that's not God's way. God wants us to look out for each other. If we are dishonest or mean, people soon find out and then they don't want to be with us or do business with us. Doing things God's way is always best.

KEY VERSE: *A person who gets ahead by oppressing the poor or by showering gifts on the rich will end in poverty. (Proverbs 22:16)*

RELATED VERSES: *Genesis 44:8; 2 Kings 5:20-27; Proverbs 10:2; 11:26; Jeremiah 17:11; Malachi 3:5; James 5:1-6*

RELATED QUESTION: *What if your boss gave you your check and he put too much money on it?*

NOTE TO PARENTS: *Encourage your children to be honest by demonstrating honesty in your own dealings with other people.*

Q: WHAT SHOULD A PERSON DO IF THE BANK MACHINE DOESN'T GIVE THE RIGHT AMOUNT OF MONEY?

99

A: If you ever get too much money from a bank machine, you should take it to the bank and explain to a teller what happened. If the machine is not near a bank, you should call the bank that owns the machine and tell them what happened. Try to give the money to whomever it belongs.

The same goes for other machines that handle money. If a pop or candy machine gives you an extra quarter, you should return the money to the people who own the machine. Machines do make mistakes, and we should try to make sure no one gets cheated as a result. God's rewards for honesty will always be greater than the money you could get from being greedy or dishonest.

KEY VERSE: *No accounting was required from the construction supervisors, because they were honest and faithful workers. (2 Kings 12:15)*

RELATED VERSES: *Genesis 44:8; Proverbs 16:11; Jeremiah 17:11*

RELATED QUESTION: *Why don't some salespeople tell the truth instead of lying?*

NOTE TO PARENTS: *Whenever you get someone else's money by mistake, try to return it to its rightful owner. Going back to a store to return extra change or to return extra money from a vending machine can make a lasting impression on a child.*

Q: WHAT IF THE WAITER GIVES ME A KID'S MEAL FREE BECAUSE HE THINKS I'M YOUNGER THAN I REALLY AM?

100

A: It is important to do what is right even if it costs you money. So if you get a children's price for a meal or a ticket and you are older than a "child," you should tell the truth. Tell the waiter, waitress, ticket seller, or whoever is in charge how old you really are. You can't put a price on honesty.

Remember that God is looking after you. He will meet all your needs and take good care of you if you do things his way. God's way is to be honest. It shows that you trust him.

KEY VERSE: *So put away all falsehood and "tell your neighbor the truth" because we belong to each other. (Ephesians 4:25)*

RELATED VERSES: *Genesis 43:20-21; 44:8; Proverbs 12:13, 17; Jeremiah 17:11*

RELATED QUESTION: *If people that lie and cheat know that they are going to lose customers later on, why do they still lie and cheat?*

Q: IS IT REALLY FINDERS KEEPERS?

A: The old saying "Finders keepers, losers weepers!" is an excuse for making no effort to return something that belongs to someone else. People usually say this when they are the finders, not the losers.

If you find something valuable, make an effort to find the owner. If you were to find a bag full of money in a parking lot, you should take it to a police station. If you find a wallet, look for a name inside and let the owner come and get it from you. If you find a ten-dollar bill in a classroom, take it to the teacher. If you find a basketball on the playground, take it to the principal. For some items, you may even want to put a note in the local paper.

On the other hand, don't worry about finding the owner of a nickel that you find in the street. It's not that valuable, and finding the owner would be practically impossible. You can keep it.

KEY VERSE: *Do for others as you would like them to do for you. (Luke 6:31)*

RELATED VERSES: *Genesis 44:8; Deuteronomy 6:1-5; Matthew 7:12; Acts 2:44-45*

RELATED QUESTION: *What if I found buried treasure?*

Q: IF I TRY TO PAY MY FRIEND BACK AND HE FORGOT I BORROWED SOME MONEY, IS IT WRONG TO KEEP IT?

102

A: If you owe somebody money, you should pay that person back, even if he or she has forgotten about the debt. You should do what is right, even if no one else knows or cares. God knows. Think about how you would feel if someone paid you back after you had forgotten. It would be a wonderful surprise, and you would think very highly of your friend.

This is the best kind of friend to have—one who looks out for you and helps you, even when he or she doesn't have to. If you are that kind of friend, you will have lots of loyal friends.

Remember, though, it's best not to borrow money. Then you never have to worry about paying your friend back.

KEY VERSE: *Do not steal. Do not cheat one another. Do not lie. (Leviticus 19:11)*

RELATED VERSES: *Exodus 22:10-15; Leviticus 19:33-34; 1 Kings 9:4-5; 2 Kings 12:15; Psalm 17:1; Jeremiah 17:11; Matthew 7:12; Luke 6:31; Acts 2:44-45; 1 Peter 2:17*

RELATED QUESTION: *What should you do if you can't return the money you borrowed?*

Q: WHY DO SOME PEOPLE TRUST ME AND LEND ME MONEY?

103

A: People usually lend money to those whom they trust. They have watched you and have come to believe in your honesty. They know you are honest because they have seen you (1) do what is right and (2) do what you say you will do.

It is good to be known as an honest person. If you do what is right and do what you say you will do, you will be known as an honest person.

KEY VERSE: *A false witness will be cut off, but an attentive witness will be allowed to speak. (Proverbs 21:28)*

RELATED VERSES: *Exodus 22:10-15; Proverbs 22:29; Ezekiel 18:16-17; Luke 16:11; 1 Timothy 3:11; 1 Peter 2:12, 16-17*

NOTE TO PARENTS: *Affirm any child for being honest. Honesty is a genuine treasure in its own right.*

Q: WHY DO SOME SALESCLERKS STEAL MONEY FROM THE CASH REGISTER?

104

A: The good news is that most salesclerks are honest and trustworthy. Otherwise they wouldn't have gotten their job in the first place. There aren't many salesclerks who steal money from cash registers.

Salesclerks who *do* steal are greedy. When they see the money in the cash register, they can't resist the temptation to steal. They give in. People who do this may try to justify what they have done by thinking that it's OK because they don't get paid very much or that the store will never miss it. But the truth is that the money is not theirs. If the boss finds out, they will lose their job.

These people don't realize that they are hurting themselves. You get more problems from dishonest money than you do from no money at all.

KEY VERSES: *Slaves [or employees] must obey their masters [or bosses] and do their best to please them. They must not talk back or steal, but they must show themselves to be entirely trustworthy and good. Then they will make the teaching about God our Savior attractive in every way. (Titus 2:9-10)*

RELATED VERSES: *Leviticus 19:35; Proverbs 13:11; Jeremiah 17:11; Habakkuk 2:12*

RELATED QUESTION: *Why do some people steal things from their company?*

Q: IS IT OK TO USE CANADIAN COINS IN AMERICAN VENDING MACHINES?

A: Many vending machines have a sign that says "No foreign coins." Money from other countries may get jammed in the machine. But even if the coins work, they may not be worth the same amount. So putting foreign coins in the machine would cheat the owner of the machine. That would be wrong.

Do not look for ways to "save money" by being dishonest. Instead, be honest all the time and trust God to take care of you. God owns everything. He can help you with the extra few cents you think you would gain from cheating the vending machine.

KEY VERSE: *The Lord despises double standards of every kind. (Proverbs 20:10)*

RELATED VERSES: *Proverbs 13:11; Jeremiah 17:11; Romans 13:1-7; 1 Peter 2:14-16*

RELATED QUESTION: *Would people know it if you photocopied money and paid for things with it?*

CHRISTIAN FINANCIAL CONCEPTS

Larry Burkett, founder and president of Christian Financial Concepts, is the best-selling author of forty-nine books on business and personal finance as well as two novels. He also hosts two radio programs broadcast on hundreds of stations worldwide.

Larry earned B.S. degrees in marketing and in finance; recently an honorary doctorate in economics was conferred on him by Southwest Baptist University. For several years he served as a manager in the space program at Cape Canaveral, Florida. He also has been vice president of an electronics manufacturing firm. Larry's education, business experience, and solid understanding of God's Word enable him to give practical, Bible-based financial counsel to families, churches, and businesses.

Founded in 1976, Christian Financial Concepts, Inc., is a nonprofit, nondenominational ministry dedicated to helping God's people gain a clear understanding of how to manage their money according to scriptural principles. Although practical assistance is provided on many levels, the purpose of CFC is simply *to bring glory to God by freeing his people from financial bondage so they may serve him to their utmost.*

One major avenue of ministry involves training volunteers in budget and debt counseling and linking them with financially troubled families and individuals through a nationwide referral network. CFC also provides financial-management seminars and workshops for churches and other groups. (Formats available include audio, video, and live instruction.) A full line of printed and audiovisual materials related to money management is available through

CFC's materials department (1-800-722-1976) or via the Internet (http://www.cfcministry.org).

Career Pathways, another outreach of Christian Financial Concepts, helps teenagers and adults find their occupational calling. The Career Pathways "assessment" gauges a person's work priorities, skills, vocational interests, and personality. Reports in each of these areas define a person's strengths, weaknesses, and unique, God-given pattern for work.

Visit CFC's Internet site at http://www.cfcministry.org or write to the address below for further information.

Christian Financial Concepts
P. O. Box 2458
Gainesville, GA 30503-2458

LIGHTWAVE PUBLISHING, INC.

Lightwave's mission is to develop quality resources and related services that encourage, assist, and equip parents to build Christian faith with their children.

Lightwave's learning resources have been sold or endorsed by such ministries as Josh McDowell Ministry, Campus Crusade for Christ, Christian Financial Concepts, the 700 Club, Living Way Ministries, and the American Family Association.

Rick and Elaine Osborne

Rick Osborne, author and speaker, encourages and teaches parents to pass on Christian faith to their children. He is the founder and president of Lightwave Publishing and Lightwave Kids Club.

Since 1984, Rick and his wife, Elaine, have been developing and producing high-quality materials that help parents teach their children about God and the Bible. Among their more than thirty books and resources are *101 Questions Children Ask about God*, *The Singing Bible*, Sticky Situations (the McGee and Me! game), and *The Adventure Bible Handbook*. Rick recently coauthored a book with Larry Burkett entitled *Financial Parenting*.

Tips and Tools

Lightwave offers a free bimonthly newsletter called *Tips and Tools for Spiritual Parenting*. This newsletter helps parents make church exciting, answer their kids' questions, and teach their children to pray. It also provides ideas for fun activities and much more. To receive a free one-year subscription, simply write to the address below to request it or call 1-800-555-9884.

Lightwave Publishing, Inc.
133
800 5th Ave., Suite 101
Seattle, WA 98104-3191

In Canada, write to:

Lightwave Publishing, Inc.
Box 160
Maple Ridge, B.C.
Canada V2X 7G1

You and your children can also visit Lightwave's Internet site at http://www.beacom.com/lw.
  Lightwave Publishing does not accept or solicit donations.